# THE ANNUITY

*From*

# MYSTERY

*To*

# MASTERY

By

Robert J. Zimmerman, M.B.A.

First published by Dog Ear Publishing
4010 W. 86th Street, Ste H
Indianapolis, IN 46268
www.dogearpublishing.net

ISBN: 1-59858-238-0

This book is printed on acid-free paper.

Printed in the United States of America

Most people can comfortably explain how a savings account works at their bank. But when asked how a savings account works at an insurance company, they are not so sure. Such is the mystique of the word—***ANNUITY.***

Similarly, many are familiar with the way mutual funds work as investments. However, if you connect those same mutual funds with an insurance company in a variable annuity, they somehow have a different aura.

Now we have a new annuity program call the 'fixed index annuity' that is being widely promoted to conservative investors. With all the variations of the basically simple concept, it is not too difficult to understand why some confusion may arise.

Without attempting to determine why the disconnect occurs, this book is an attempt to lead to a better understanding of the unique aspects of annuities that make them so valuable a planning tool for each of us. It is also hoped that some of the examples given in the book will cause people to take another look at their existing annuities, and see if they can find a way to make them work harder.

For those who have had an idea of making a charity part of their planning, there are ideas presented that illustrate how this can be done more easily, and also accomplished without necessarily disinheriting their own family.

Recognizing that not everybody will agree with the observations presented here, the author nevertheless is adamant in his disagreement with the naysayers who criticize annuities. Hopefully this book will help the reader come to a fresh understanding of annuities on their own merits.

If you harbor a prejudice against annuities, perhaps this book will assist you to do the 'right thing' in making your financial arrangements. In spite of all the negative comments you will hear elsewhere regarding annuities, having access to the whole story will be enlightening, and will allow you to take advantage of what knowledgeable investors have known for a long time.

# TABLE OF CONTENTS

# ACKNOWLEDGMENTS:

To my beloved wife, Kathy, for her willingness to proof read my copy and make sure I did not get carried away with 'insurance speak'.

To all the investment writers covering insurance plans and annuities who motivated me to speak up.

To Denise Grace, for her generous commitment of time and professional editing experience.

To all my peers in the industry who encouraged me to make an effort to educate the public.

# INTRODUCTION

Despite the fact that we are living in "The Age of Information," it is a definite challenge for most people to garner the knowledge they need to establish an informed plan of any kind to meet their financial goals.

When people are asked in polite conversation "What do you know about annuities?" the response typically is a shrug of the shoulders or something similar. Most people are aware of the fact that they are contracts issued by an insurance company. That seems to lead to a general letdown of mental function, and sometimes a totally negative response. Their negativity can usually be traced to something that they read in the financial section of a newspaper or perhaps on the internet.

If your use of annuities has been restricted by the mystique of insurance company jargon, or if you have the idea fostered by many in the news media that annuities are only for investing neophytes, then it is hoped that some of the ideas I will offer in this book will be helpful to you.

The so-called experts do little or nothing to explain this longstanding financial planning tool, and it is a challenge to determine whether these commentators have a built in agenda or are just plain ill-informed. It is a rarity to find a financial guru who has anything nice to say about annuities. A strong case can be made that they cost their followers a lot of money.

Contrary to what the critics proclaim, educated and informed investors have made great use of annuities over the years. An understanding of the features and benefits available with annuities gives evidence of the fact that they offer answers to the major concerns of most investors. Undoubtedly, alternatives to annuities have their advantages. However, it is not necessary to abandon those benefits in order to take advantage of what annuities offer.

This book could be called "Everything you wanted to know about annuities, but were afraid to ask!" But that implies that the author has all the knowledge. Truth be told, that is not the case! Many years of experience have yielded sufficient ideas to share, and anyone who cares to read and research what is said in these pages can be well rewarded financially.

The aim of this work, then, is to not only clarify, but also to allow people who own annuities, or are considering investing in them, to maximize their value. Even if you have an animosity toward anything the insurance industry has to offer, by taking the time to explore with us the alternatives available to you, you indicate an openness to learn, and that is all that can be asked.

Who, then, should invest the time to read this work? You should do so if:

- You already own annuities, for the reasons stated in the prior paragraph.
- You are considering placing money in an annuity account.
- You are a financial advisor, and recognize that there is always something to learn.

The goal of all financial planning is to enhance peace of mind by minimizing money related worries. Insurance and annuities are magnificent tools to facilitate this goal. By becoming a knowledgeable investor, you can eliminate the fear factor, and avoid surprises later.

# CHAPTER 1

# WHAT IS AN ANNUITY?

Anyone who has seen the movie <u>Fantasia</u> can readily remember the scene showing Mickey Mouse as the sorcerer's apprentice. Carrying unending buckets of water, the sorcerer is not able to turn off the water flow and the final scene shows a flood.

If you change the cargo that Mickey is transporting from water to cash, you can readily understand what an annuity is all about. Visualize a bucket of cash arriving in your mailbox or bank account for as long as you live, and you have an idea of what annuities are designed to do. Unlike the sorcerer, you do not want to stop Mickey in his task. You want that income to keep on flooding into your account.

If you look up the meaning of *annuity* in a dictionary, you will find that it is a "specified income payable at stated intervals for a fixed or contingent period, often for the recipient's life, in consideration of a premium paid."

Quite so! To give you a choice, here is another definition: " An annuity is a certificate of deposit with an insurance company that pays a higher rate of interest than a bank certificate, allows you to defer taxes on income you do not use, and offers a variety of payouts that you cannot outlive."

Most people think of an annuity as a contract issued by an insurance company, but there is also such a thing as a 'private annuity'. In this instance, the obligation to make good on the agreement rests with an individual or other non-insurance entity.

Is the value of a lifetime income becoming more acknowledged by the planning community? This fact was recently called "the longevity risk" by a representative of one of the largest mutual fund organizations in the world. In other words—too much life left over at the end of the money! This is the risk that is addressed by using annuities.

Annuities are pretty imposing documents for most people, and thus they have become one of the least read best sellers. After all, who has the time to become familiar with all the jargon—even though it has a direct impact on one's financial well being?

All insurance contracts should be viewed as property. They are financial assets that can be compared to real assets, such as homes and automobiles. An annuity is an income producing asset. Think of it as real property, like a rental house. Unlike a rental home, however, you have no tenant problems or other management concerns.

Annuities are *safe money* investments. The source of their safety is discussed in the following chapter. While it may be surprising to many, even Variable Annuities can be categorized as safe money, simply because of the guarantees that are not available with alternative investments. While annuities may be appropriate for those with a long-term outlook, there are some variables that cater to those who need total liquidity. In other words, no surrender charges.

Not to be confused with annuities, a Life Insurance plan can be looked upon as a certificate of deposit for your heirs. It is an estate asset that can be acquired at a substantial discount. In addition, for senior citizens who enjoy good health, there are insurance plans available that make other forms of investments take a back seat. Such insurance plans are designed for those seeking to create a legacy for their heirs or their favorite charity.

There is a saying; "If you don't know the merchandise, know the merchant." That certainly applies to the idea of dealing with insurance. If you go to buy a diamond, you are comforted in knowing the person who is selling it. Most people cannot tell the difference between a diamond and a cubic zirconium.

In spite of the fact that some insurance salespeople have found it necessary to use pressure sales tactics, it sure is nice when you can find one who can be trusted to give honest counsel that ties in with your financial interests and objectives. More and more, you will find that the representative you speak with will be well informed and conscientious. Insurance companies do not care to have their names associated with any abuse.

Over the years, it has been rewarding for many agents to witness the actual performance of insurance contracts when they are needed. In spite of the credibility gap some people experience when dealing with insurance, most people are very grateful to have had the foresight to have the insurance in place when needed. Indeed, some even take the time to express thanks to the person who helped them set it up. This is the motivation that enables the insurance professional to have continued endurance in his or her task in the face of client doubts and efforts to procrastinate.

So, remember, when you must put up with a lengthy explanation of any insurance contract, it is only because the agent is trying to do a complete and honest job. He/She has a valid program to offer, but it is a definite plus for both parties to have a full understanding of just what it does and does not cover. It is good for each party to avoid surprises.

# CHAPTER 2

# HOW MOST PEOPLE KNOW ANNUITIES

Most people are aware that there are *Annuities* and *Variable Annuities*, but are not quite sure what the difference is. This chapter will focus primarily on the *Fixed Annuity*, as there will be a separate chapter on *Variables*, and one dealing with a relatively new form of fixed annuity called a *Fixed Index Annuity*.

While many annuities are set up with a single deposit, you can also establish an account that allows you to add money on a regular basis. This is called a *flexible payment annuity*, and it is a useful way for those seeking to build capital over a period of time. Single payment annuities are typically used for transferring a block of money to a place better suited for long-term needs, with the idea of using these funds at a future date.

It is interesting to note how some people have come to understand annuities. One client, in a recent a discussion of annuities, made the remark, "I already have an annuity!" Where did he get the idea that annuities were being rationed out? Do banks allow just one account? It reminds one of a suggestion made for a birthday present for a seventh grader—the gift of a book. His retort was, "I already have a book!"

And then there was the 70 year old who wondered if he was *too old* for an annuity. There are some folks who question the use of annuities for seniors altogether, as if people who are older no longer have a need for a safe way to manage their nest egg.

If you would like to know if you are a candidate to put your savings into an annuity, here are some helpful hints:

- You wish to earn a higher interest rate than you are presently receiving on your CD

- You are looking for a stable rate of return that is free from risk of stock market decline

- You are not in need of the interest for dividend earnings for current income

- You would like to take advantage of the power of tax deferral on your interest

- You want to avoid double taxation of your social security

- You like having your nest egg free of the probate system and potential creditors

- You want to allocate funds for long-term needs

Even after listening to a salesperson list the benefits of owning annuities, most people will soon forget or dismiss the essential features. So, as a memory jogger, here is a review of those features that make annuities an important building block in any financial plan.

# SAFETY

Return *OF* your money trumps return *ON* your money. That is what *safety* is all about! Any discussion of safety should be preceded by this understanding: There is no such thing as *a risk free* investment! Without a doubt, there are varying degrees of risk, but there are NO investments that are *risk free*. It is just a matter of knowing what degree of risk is involved.

Usually the money placed in annuities is *nest egg* money. When you are talking about nest eggs, the assumption is that these eggs are not to be scrambled, but should always be sunny side up.

Even when you bury the money in a tin can in your yard or put it under your mattress, there is the obvious risk of theft, or physical destruction. Beyond that, there is the risk of inflation. If you go to the mattress for the cash you stored there, the dollars you put away ten years ago will not buy the same amount of groceries, gasoline or postage stamps in today's marketplace.

Most people are aware of the fact that banks offer something called FDIC to protect their account. FDIC stands for Federal Deposit Insurance Corporation, and it protects an account up to $100,000 if the bank fails. FDIC is an insurance company, yet few people bother to ask what happens if it fails.

One of the first places one thinks of to put *safe money* is likely to be in government bonds. Yet, like every other choice, there are risks involved even with these *safe* holdings. The first one that comes to mind is the risk of inflation. The question you need to ask is: will your money buy the same amount of goods as when you made the original investment?

There is also the risk of loss of principal if you liquidate prior to the bond's maturity date. Bonds are quoted in the financial section of the paper, and that means that they fluctuate in value. If you bought a long term bond that yielded 4% a couple of years ago, and current yields are 6%, you will find that your principal has gone down if you need to liquidate before the bonds reach their maturity date. (Why would anyone pay full price for your 4% bond when they can buy one with a current yield of 6%?)

Insurance companies can invest in the same bonds, in fact, they do. You may be familiar with the term Legal Reserve Life Insurance Company. This refers to the fact that insurance companies maintain reserves at least equal to the minimum prescribed by law or regulation in the state in which it does business. These reserves are based on actuarial formulas and are designed to allow the company to meet all of its financial obligations. Also, the laws require maintenance of certain levels of capital and surplus to provide additional protection to policyholders.

Those same investments are the source of the earnings you see credited to your annuity account. Your money is part of the insurance company's general account which is its asset base. The safety of your investment is directly related to their general financial strength. It is not the same for Variable Annuities, though. With Variable Annuities, your funds are invested in sub-accounts (Mutual Funds) which are kept separate from the insurer's general account. Those accounts may fluctuate with the securities markets, but are generally immune to the insurance company's overall financial situation.

With a *fixed* annuity, the insurance company accepts the market risk—not you. This is similar to the position of the bank that pays you interest. Their investments can fluctuate in the market but it does not affect the amount of interest you have contracted with them to receive. Because insurance companies are involved with longer term obligations, they can make longer term investments which typically carry higher yields. These yields are then passed along to their account holders.

These longer term holdings are also subject to market risk if liquidated prior to maturity. Some of the annuities you will consider will share that market risk with you. You will see it referred to as Market Value Adjustment, or MVA. It typically applies only when your account is closed during the surrender period. By offering you more favorable annuity terms, the insurance company asks you to share the burden of some of the *market risk* in exchange.

If the insurance companies run into financial problems with their investments, your account does not enjoy FDIC protection. All the annuity promotional material you will see now will have that fact displayed in bold type to any potential investor.

One can rightly ask: Why would anyone put their savings in a noninsured account? There must be a good reason, because every year billions of dollars are transferred to annuities, with much of that transfer taking place in the lobbies of banks themselves.

Each state offers up to $100,000 protection for annuities from a state established guaranty fund that is backed up by contributions from all companies selling annuities in that state. This is not something you will see in their advertising or sales presentations, but it exists in every state and it should be comforting for the annuity holder to know about. There are some states that offer even higher limits.

What typically happens, though, is that the troubled company is swallowed up by a larger company which makes good on the accounts. This has helped some of the larger companies increase their size, while at the same time making the client whole. It has also been a great public relations benefit for the industry. The practicality of it is that you will have to look long and hard to find anyone who has lost their principal in an annuity account because of an insurance company failure.

Your home is a major asset. You automobile could cause major financial loss due to an accident. You properly use insurance companies to protect yourself from loss. Do you scrutinize the companies you deal with for these needs to see if they have the ability to pay when their benefits are needed? If not, why would you treat the company offering you annuities any differently?

Someone recently made the remark that he knew of a risk free investment. He advised, "Invest in taxes—they always go up!" Of course, the retort was, "Yes, they are a guaranteed investment—a guaranteed loss!" Many people, however, do invest in taxes by simply paying more than the law requires. The information in this book is designed to help solve this problem by making you aware of the advantages of tax control offered by annuity accounts. (Would you miss having all those 1099 tax forms to deal with every year?)

# TAX ADVANTAGES

One of your guarantees with a bank account is the guarantee of tax-ation of your interest, even if you do not use it. Annuities have the advantage of allowing your interest to accumulate on a 'tax deferred' basis. So, instead of receiving a 1099 tax form every year for interest that is earned (but not spent), you can have that interest re-invested in the account, and this compounds over the years to allow the value of the annuity to grow in a sheltered environment.

Salespeople will point out that this allows you to earn interest three ways:

- Interest on your principal
- Interest on your interest
- Interest on the taxes you did not pay.

There will come a time, however, when you will need to withdraw funds from the account, and that is when you get the tax bill. This gives rise to the objection of many experts who say that clients are better advised to pay taxes as they go along. If this thinking were car-ried out logically, no one would ever see fit to put money into IRA and 401K accounts, as one of their main advantages is tax deferral on earnings.

Here is another way to look at it: If a banker would loan you money interest free for 10 years, and then only require you to return the orig-inal loan, how much would you borrow? If you put a pencil to it, you would take every dime he would lend you. You could simply take the earnings over the 10 years and give him his principal back at the end of the term. When you can get tax deferment on your earned interest, it is just like getting a loan from the IRS.

If you prefer to place money in a CD yielding 4% and pay the tax currently, your return on that account will not only be diminished by the taxes you will pay, but also by the hidden tax called inflation as we have previously discussed. When you factor in taxes and loss of purchasing power due to inflation, your principal is fortunate to remain intact.

Sometimes we hear that there is no point in deferring taxes because you will have to pay up someday. That is mathematically false reasoning, even if you compute the highest tax brackets. (See Appendix IV). It also erroneously supposes that you liquidate the entire annuity at one time—what is sometimes referred to as *taxicide*. When it comes time to take out the money, most people do so in the form of an income stream, not in a lump sum. The exception would be the heirs who typically cannot wait to spend their inheritance. It is up to them to deal with the taxes. In a later chapter, we will point out a way to deal with the deferred tax that has accumulated over the life of the account, and we will share with you the actual case history of a lady who put her trust in annuities.

There is another tax consideration that comes into play for many retirees. That is the tax on social security income. Many senior citizens are surprised to find that they now must pay income tax on their social security income. If income is over $25,000 for one person, or over $34,000 for a couple, 50% of the amount received will be taxed. If income exceeds $32,000 for an individual, or $44,000 for a couple, then 85% of the social security income is taxable under current laws.

However, the good news is that many can plan their affairs to avoid having this income subjected to income tax. Interest income from bank accounts, and even interest income from tax free bonds are counted in tallying up your total income. Interest from annuities, however, does *not* count in the calculation as long as it is left in the account. This allows seniors an opportunity to do some planning if they wish to utilize annuities for their financial goals.

For those folks looking to do some tax planning, it is interesting to note that there is now a program called a ROTH IRA account that offers tax sheltered earnings on investments inside the accounts.

Roth accounts allow no deductibility from current income for money transferred into the account. In that it allows tax-free investment growth, and does not have a required withdrawal deadline like a regular IRA or 401K plan; a Roth account works much like an annuity. Annuities, however, have at least two advantages over Roth IRA's:

- No contribution limits

- No restrictions on how soon you can start withdrawals (Special rules apply prior to age 59 1/2)

The decision to elect to pay taxes currently rather than in the future is one that assumes both your income and tax rates will be higher in the future, and that it is a better strategy to pay tax today at the lower rates than rates that may be effective in a decade or two. There are those who say that paying taxes at current rates is a no brainer, because the IRS will be taxing all those IRA and 401K accounts at tax rates that have been impacted not only by higher health care costs, but also the accumulated fiscal problems of prior generations. It is certainly something to think about for those who will be needing the funds for income in the future.

## HIGHER EARNINGS

You may notice that when comparing the interest rates offered by a bank CD with the rates credited to annuities, that the annuities typically pay 1% or more higher. Not only that, a certificate of annuity will also give you a guaranteed minimum interest rate to be credited over the life of the account—something you cannot expect from a bank certificate.

The reason this is true is that insurance companies are in a position to make longer term investments which normally have higher yields. When your annuity contract is issued, the insurance company takes on a long term obligation to offer you an income that you cannot outlive. (Remember, you are advised to consider annuities as long term planning tools.)

Normally, if you need to have ready access to the funds for any reason, you would not use an annuity. There is an exception to that which we will mention in the chapter on Variable Annuities. Many companies offer annuities that are 100% free of a surrender charge. In that chapter, you will also see how you can directly influence the earnings capabilities of your annuity account.

# A PROBATE-FREE PLAN

The subject of avoiding the probate system is too broad to include in this work. For our purpose, it can be merely observed that there is no probate procedure involved in transferring annuity accounts to your heirs—no fees, no publicity, no delays, and no contestability. The reason your annuity does not go through probate is simply this: Annuities, like Life Insurance, allow you to name the beneficiary of the account. The insurance company must follow your instructions and it is not necessary to have a probate judge drop the gavel and approve this arrangement. It is automatic and accepted.

Care should be taken when naming beneficiaries. You should name contingent beneficiaries or you could name your trust as the beneficiary. If there is no named beneficiary alive when the claim is presented to the insurance company, then you will find your account becomes grist for the probate mill.

A probate judge must approve assets transferred under a will. Wills do not take effect until proven in court. Most people are not aware of this until they actually experience the process.

# SURRENDER CHARGES

No discussion of annuities, whether fixed or variable, is complete without mention of surrender charges. All companies now require a client to sign a statement of understanding about the account, and that includes the matter of surrender charges.

People sometimes have a problem with surrender charges for annuities, even when they do not have a problem with charges made by a bank. While a bank imposes a charge for early surrender each time a certificate is rolled over, insurance companies makes a charge at the beginning and it reduces over the years and then goes away completely.

A surrender charge is a benefit to all that do not take their long term investment early. It allows the insurance company to provide higher benefits to the *stay the distance* investor.

When you receive your annuity statement from the company, there will be a line that says 'Annuitization Value' or 'Account Value.' That is the value on which your earnings are calculated while the annuity is at work. There will also be a line which says 'Cash Value' or 'Surrender Value.' That is that amount you will receive if you change your mind and close (surrender) the account. The difference between the account value and the cash value is a direct reflection of the surrender charge schedule you received when you opened the account.

Discussion of these charges brings up the question of the need for liquidity. Most people have an emotional response to this perceived need, one not largely based on fact. If total liquidity is required, the correct solution is to simply place the money in a lower yielding account that gives 100% penalty free access. You can expect lower earnings on this type of account. That is your trade-off.

As previously mentioned, insurance companies make long-term investment decisions. When a client changes their mind, the insurance company incurs a loss to liquidate. Surrender charges help offset that cost, and all other expenses involved in setting up the account.

Most companies allow access to 10% of your account each year without penalty, and they do not typically impose charges when you elect a payout option. Many annuities have a provision to waive surrender charges for those entering a nursing home or finding themselves in a terminal illness situation.

Both fixed and variable annuities are recommended as long-term financial alternatives. They are not intended to be used as "put and take" accounts. Banks are the proper place for such funds.

This notion is reinforced by another charge that comes along with annuities—one that is imposed by the laws of the land. Like IRA accounts, there is a penalty imposed for annuity withdrawals prior to age 59 1/2. For such withdrawals, the IRS levies a 10% federal excise tax, and in addition you will pay ordinary income tax on any gains. It simply gives witness to the fact that annuities are intended to be a source of income in retirement years.

There are exceptions to the 59 1/2 age limit, and a competent agent will be able to show you the ropes. For now, you are well advised to think of the age restriction as a benefit. Tax sheltered earnings are a *carrot* and the IRS restrictions are a *stick* to keep you on the path of saving for your retirement.

# BONUS ANNUITIES

Many companies have a program which is designed to help a client offset surrender charges that may be incurred if they move money from an existing account, whether it be a bank, mutual fund or another company's annuity. Your account is credited with a bonus amount which is stated up front. The bonus applies even if there are no liquidation or surrender costs incurred with the account that is being moved.

Naturally, these bonuses come with a price if you withdraw early, usually an increase in the surrender charge period for the new account. If you change your mind, you will not only give back the bonus, you will incur the normal surrender charge. You can look upon a bonus annuity as a loan made to you by the insurance company to induce you to become their long-term customer. It makes sense for them to take back the bonus if you change your mind about the account and elect to leave.

When setting up a Variable Annuity, and are considering accepting a bonus, you should ask yourself this question: Will the selection of investment choices offered satisfy my investment needs over the long term? In other words, if the investment world outside the Variable Annuity offers nothing better than what is offered with the annuity, why would you change your account? Why not take the bonus?

# PAYOUT CHOICES

Since an income payout is the avowed purpose of annuities in the first place, there will be a separate chapter devoted to the subject. For now, let us examine a few generalities.

If you set up an annuity account to start paying you a regular check from the beginning, you have what is called an Immediate Annuity. This is also referred to as the *payout stage*. If you do not want to have the income start right away, you have what is called a Deferred Annuity—the funds accumulate in the account to be used later. This is known as the *accumulation stage*.

You may recall that the sales person told you that you would be given choices when the time came to get your money back. Aside from the choice of taking a lump sum, you could elect a payout over a fixed number of years, or for a fixed amount periodically until the account was used up.

The most appropriate choice for most people is to have the income stream guaranteed for life—like a pension. That is the thing that insurance companies are good at. They are used to dealing with mortality tables, and can give you a lifetime guarantee that banks and mutual funds do not offer.

You should be encouraged to use annuities as soon as possible to generate regular income, even when you do not need the money for current living expenses. The reason for this will be elaborated on in a later chapter, and we will comment more extensively on the use of payout alternatives, and how to make that annuity account perform to maximize your financial goals

# WHO ARE THE PLAYERS?

Before going any further, let us make sure that we know the distinction between the parties to an annuity account:

- The Insurance Company

- The Owner

- The Beneficiary

- The Annuitant

This information should be covered by the representative who helps set up the account, but like much of the other information you receive, it is commonly understood and then forgotten. Here is a brief reminder:

The Owner: The person who controls all the decisions. Ownership could be shared with another person who would be the co-owner. Think of the bank savings account you have—you are the owner. If it is a jointly held account, you are the co-owner.

The Annuitant: The person who will receive the payout if you decide to turn the account into an income stream. Typically, this would be you, the owner, but it also could be another person who is designated by the owner.

The Beneficiary: The person or persons who are designated to receive the account value on the death the owner. The designation can be made irrevocable if you so decide. A contingent beneficiary can also be named. That beneficiary would be the recipient of the funds if there was no primary beneficiary alive at the time of the passing of the owner.

Care should be taken when the annuity is set up as the designations you elect are binding on the insurance company. Failure to properly name beneficiaries could have unanticipated effects, and the whole challenge in advising clients is to avoid surprises. (*See the later chapter on avoiding surprises*.) Just as important as it is with Life Insurance, you should use the contingent beneficiary option made available with annuities.

If the death benefit is paid as a result of the death of the owner, then the annuity is said to be *owner* driven. If the benefit is paid on the death of the annuitant, then the annuity is said to be *annuitant* driven. This is only significant if the owner and annuitant are different persons. Most annuities are owner driven, but you should validate this if there is a separate owner and annuitant.

# TAX SHELTERED ANNUITIES

Over the years, many have become familiar with Tax Sheltered Annuities (TSA) through their place of employment. They are set up under the names of 403b or 457 plans, referring to the applicable sections of the IRS code. Like the well known IRA and 401k programs, they allow an employee to set aside money from current earnings and defer payment of income taxes until they retire.

Often times you hear a criticism of using annuities in IRA's or 401k plans. The critics say, "Why place a tax shelter inside a tax shelter?" Isn't it interesting that you seldom hear the same criticism leveled at TSA programs? It would seem that the problem would be as applicable to one as to the other.

# MEDICAID ANNUITIES

Some insurance companies offer a specialized annuity plan that is designed to enable you to devise a way to qualify for Medicaid as a solution to the problem of paying for long term nursing home stays.

Most annuities that can be liquidated count toward the Medicaid asset limit. The so-called "Medicaid Annuity" is NOT counted toward the Medicaid asset limit because it is irrevocable and it cannot be transferred or assigned.

If you are told to invest in an annuity contract that locks up your assets to the point that they are not available to you, other than as an income flow, even when in a family emergency, in an amount that places your assets below the level of government assistance, think twice!! Laws change, and vary from state to state. What if your children come into financial trouble, to the point that you want to help them? What if the government cracks down on this practice, as has been threatened?

Many annuities provide a guaranteed early penalty free withdrawal should you find it necessary to enter a nursing home or suffer a terminal illness.

## A LESSER KNOWN FEATURE

You seldom hear this mentioned as a benefit, but in a number of states, the funds you have invested in annuities cannot be taken away from you in a lawsuit. The laws of this vary with the state of your residence, but in this age of lawsuit conscious public, it should be a comfort to you to be able to take advantage of this benefit if you can. Check with your legal advisor to see if your state laws have a provision that governs this.

# CHAPTER 3

# FIXED INDEX ANNUITIES

"How would you like to invest in an account that goes up when the stock market goes up, but does not go down when the stock market goes down?"

This is a question likely to be asked when you talk to an annuity salesperson these days. What he is talking about is commonly known as a Fixed Indexed Annuity (FIA). While this may sound like a Variable Annuity to you, it is really a Fixed Annuity. Formerly known as 'equity indexed annuities', we have seen a change in nomenclature to refer to them as Fixed Index Annuities (FIA) to avoid confusing these annuities with stock market investments.

An FIA is merely a way to allow your interest rate to be sweetened because it is determined by the performance of a market index such as the Dow Jones Industrial Average or the S & P 500 index. Put another way, your interest rate is determined by the variance in the index used. It is not to be construed as being invested directly in the stock market simply because the interest credits are linked to a stock market index.

Recently a bank came forth with a Certificate of Deposit that has a link to the stock market similar to the FIA. It uses a similar crediting method as described above, but it suffers the same tax defect as all bank accounts—no shelter of interest earnings that annuities offer, plus several of the other features that are unique to annuities as described in the previous chapter.

If the idea of stock market gains with no stock market losses sounds too good to be true, let us take a second look at how it can be done. You can actually make up your own plan. All you need to know is when you expect to get your principal returned to you.

Let us say you want your funds returned in five years. If you know that you can lock in a 4.5% interest rate for five years, you can mathematically compute how much to invest today in order to guarantee that value in five years. For every dollar to be delivered you need only invest approximately 80 cents, and that leaves you 20 cents to invest elsewhere.

Now, if you invest this 20 cents in some way in the stock market, whatever it earns over the next 5 years, gets added to your account. If the stock market goes to the floor, you still will have your principal returned. (You can do the same if you invest it at the horse races, in which case you would call it your guaranteed racetrack account.)

If you set up a fixed annuity with a rate locked in for five years, and a separate annuity that has a stock market component *(see the chapter on Variable Annuities)* you will have established your own version of a Fixed Indexed Annuity plan.

If you do so, you can forget all the complicated formulas that are present with FIA accounts. With any FIA program out there, you will be told about *caps, spread, averaging and participation rates,* etc. In other words, there are a lot of moving parts, and if you think it is confusing, consider the plight of the agent whose job is to explain it to you.

# TERMS TO UNDERSTAND

With all the components that go into calculating the amount of interest credits you will receive, you should have some understanding of the terms you will encounter. We will give it our best shot, and then will tell you the one most important thing to look for. Most companies will use one, or a combination of these features. Here goes:

Cap—a maximum percentage limit on earnings. If you have an 8% cap, that is the most interest that will be credited to your account, even if the market goes up 50%. All companies have such caps. Some guarantee they will not drop below a specified figure.

Participation Rate—the percent of the index increase that your account is credited. If you have a 60% participation rate and the index goes up 15%, your share is 9% (unless there is a *cap*). Caveat: Some companies will guarantee your participation rate and some will not.

Spread—sometimes called an *asset fee*, this is the amount deducted from the index yield. (A 2% spread means that if the index increases 10%, your account will be credited 8%). There are some contracts that guarantee that no spread will be charged.

Averaging—a modifier that tends to smooth the effect of both increases and decreases in the index being used. It could be a monthly average or an annual average.

Floor—the minimum interest rate that will be credited to your account. Usually this will be applied to just 90% of the amount you invest.

Index period—also referred to at the *term*, it is the length of time from the date you start your account to the time the insurance company is liable to account to you.

Point to point method—credits interest by comparing the index at the start of the index period with the index value at the end.

High Water Mark—looks back to the highest anniversary value to compute the gain for the index period.

As you can imagine, there is potential for a lot of confusion when you go to compare various methodologies. Add in the volatility of the stock market, and you have the potential for considerable confusion. (A well known expert has written a book about these annuities that is over 200 pages).

There is a saving grace, however, that is not mentioned above, and that is called the

# ANNUAL RESET OF PRINCIPAL

We suggest that the first thing to look for in analyzing an FIA is this: Does it include a provision to reset the contractual guarantee on an annual basis? You can ignore the caps, spreads and participation limits, but not the reset feature. You will find that most annuities include a provision for annual reset, but some have a reset every other year.

When examining hypotheticals, keep in mind that it is possible to construct a favorable performance scenario for past years with any structural methodology you use. You can make a case for just about any of them if you select the proper time frame. The problem is this: nobody can predict what the next year or the next five years will be for the index you are using. That is why the annual reset is so significant. You want to know that whatever gains you achieve will not be given back in the following year. Preservation of principal is the issue. With the annual reset, you get a fresh start on your principal guarantee on every anniversary of your account.

A stock market investor who rode the index starting from the year 2001 was on a wild downhill ride. If his account saw a 50% reduction in value, it will take those funds 9 years to get back to where they were, if he has an average gain of 8% per year. A 6% rate of return would take 12 years to get back to where they started.

We have constructed a fictional interest crediting method based on the Dow Jones index for the year 2005. This is strictly a hypothetical illustration to show you how resetting works. The account will be credited with the increase each month, and in those months where the index went down, the account value will receive ZERO interest credit—i.e., it will not go down. (That's the feature of FIA's—remember?)

Following are the index quotes for the 1st trading dates of each month of 2005 for the Dow:

|          | Index Value | % Change |
|----------|-------------|----------|
| Jan. 1   | 10803       |          |
| Feb. 1   | 10523       | -2.59%   |
| Mar. 1   | 10795       | 2.58%    |
| Apr. 1   | 10551       | -2.26%   |
| May 1    | 10236       | -2.99%   |
| June 1   | 10466       | 2.25%    |
| July 1   | 10304       | -1.55%   |
| Aug. 1   | 10667       | 3.52%    |
| Sept. 1  | 10557       | -1.03%   |
| Oct. 1   | 10541       | -0.15%   |
| Nov. 1   | 10454       | -0.83%   |
| Dec. 1   | 10861       | 3.80%    |
| Dec. 31  | 10717       | -1.23%   |

The closing index at year's end was lower than the starting index, and this means that there would have been a ZERO interest credit for the year if you were on the annual point-to-point system. Monthly averaging would have the same result. Using a fresh start of principal on a 'monthly reset' program would result in over a 12% interest credit to the account. Can you understand the importance of this feature? Here is how a $10,000 account would look:

|         | Index Value | % Change | Interest Credited | Account Balance |
|---------|-------------|----------|-------------------|-----------------|
| Jan. 1  | 10803       |          |                   | 10,000          |
| Feb. 1  | 10523       | -2.59%   | 0.00%             | 10,000          |
| Mar. 1  | 10795       | 2.58%    | 2.58%             | 10,258          |
| Apr. 1  | 10551       | -2.26%   | 0.00%             | 10,258          |
| May 1   | 10236       | -2.99%   | 0.00%             | 10,258          |
| June 1  | 10466       | 2.25%    | 2.25%             | 10,489          |
| July 1  | 10304       | -1.55%   | 0.00%             | 10,489          |
| Aug. 1  | 10667       | 3.52%    | 3.52%             | 10,858          |
| Sept. 1 | 10557       | -1.03%   | 0.00%             | 10,858          |
| Oct. 1  | 10541       | -0.15%   | 0.00%             | 10,858          |
| Nov. 1  | 10454       | -0.83%   | 0.00%             | 10,858          |
| Dec. 1  | 10861       | 3.80%    | 3.80%             | 11,271          |
| Dec. 31 | 10717       | -1.23%   | 0.00%             | 11,271          |
|         |             |          |                   | 12.71%          |

You will notice that there were only 4 months where there was an increase in the index, and 8 months where it dropped. Notice that in the months where the index went down, the account balance remained unchanged. When the index went up, the account balance was credited to reflect the growth for that month.

The illustration demonstrates what can happen with fluctuations in the market using various crediting methods. Two methods would have produced 0% return, and one produced over 12%.

If you are an advocate of direct index fund investing, you will have a hard time competing with the FIA because you do not have the advantage of annually resetting the principal. You are at the mercy of the vagaries of the market, whichever direction it takes. You may have a nice year one year and give back your gain in the following year.

Let us say that you had a five year point-to-point crediting method during the five year period from January 1, 1998 to Dec. 31, 2002.

Here are actual index figures found for the most commonly used index, the S & P 500:

Jan. 1, 1998            975

Dec. 31, 2002          880

At the end of five years, the index was lower than the starting point. Your interest credit for 5 years is ZERO. It is no consolation to know that the index actually reached as high as 1500 during that five year term. It went up 31% in 1998, and nearly 15% in 1999. The index was down three out of the five years.

If you had an index annuity with a *point to point* method in that time period, you would not be in a loss position with your account—you would just have received ZERO interest earnings. However, with an FIA annual reset provision, your account would be worth over 50% more than you had deposited, even with a zero return for three out of five years. What better demonstration of the power of an FIA with an annual reset methodology?

Admittedly, a unique time period has been selected to demonstrate the point. This has been done to illustrate why so many people have placed serious money with FIA accounts. However, since the interest credits can be zero in a down market, do not forget what the insurance company told you ahead of time.

If you want to avoid a zero year, you can instruct the company to place some of your funds in their guaranteed interest option—a choice they all offer. And, you typically can re-allocate your account on each anniversary. So, if your crystal ball tells you the market will go down in the next year, you can tell the company to put all or part of your money in the 'fixed' interest account.

Trying to outguess the market keeps even the professional money managers challenged. If you have funds that cannot be subjected to stock market losses and that are intended for future income needs, the FIA is a good way to have a chance to participate in the upside potential of the overall stock market without jeopardizing your principal. For many folks, they are certainly a worthy piece in the planning puzzle. Since their introduction in the 1990's these contracts have met with increasing acceptance by the public. They remember well what the stock market did after 2001.

Included in Appendix three of this book is a BUYER'S GUIDE TO FIXED INDEX ANNUITIES. It is a very complete guide if you wish to become fully comfortable with your decision in this continually changing environment.

Like the traditional *fixed* annuity, the index annuities can be looked on as a *safe money* investment. If you put money into a fixed interest account or a bank CD, and the stock market soars, you will not participate in that growth. That leaves you wondering if you have missed an opportunity. On the other hand, if you put money in a stock market investment, and the market flops, you will regret that decision.

With the Fixed Index Annuity, you have an excellent alternative. Within one account, you can have the potential of high returns available in the stock market and the security of having your principal guaranteed. In other words, there is no need to choose between greater risk or greater safety. In the same account, you can have both safety and opportunity.

# CHAPTER 4

# WHAT ABOUT VARIABLE ANNUITIES?

I n our review of fixed annuities, it should come through that the key word to describe these accounts ought to be:

## GUARANTEES

They are basically a form of savings account, intended for *safe money*. When it comes to Variable Annuities (VA), you should change the key word to:

## OPPORTUNITY plus GUARANTEES

It is not necessary to give up guarantees, but most people use variables for those funds you wish to make grow in the securities markets. If you look at brochures for VA's, they all seem to concentrate on their ability to build accounts by offering a variety of professional money managers to manage your money inside their 'annuity wrapper'.

We have commented that while there is a link to the stock market performance with Fixed Index Annuities, they do have a limited ability to participate fully. You have either a cap or a percentage participation in an index. You do not have the ability to direct your investments as you would do if you were to invest in a family of mutual funds. They are basically a *safe money* variation from the traditional fixed annuity format.

There is nothing wrong with this if you are apt to be a conservative investor and understand the limitations along with the advantages. As a part of an overall program, they do nicely. However, you should also know there is an added way to take advantage of what annuities have to offer. If you want to have more action for any part of your nest egg, you can look to a Variable Annuity as a way to jump into the stock market.

Speaking of jumping, you may have a recollection of a photograph showing a man walking on a high wire strung between two skyscrapers, with no safety net. That is the image of many people who respond to the suggestion of putting money into anything related to the stock market. They see it as high risk opportunity to achieve financial meltdown when the stock market plunges.

If you take that high wire act and slide a net about one foot under the wire, it changes the risk picture substantially. In fact, with such a safety net, you might be able to do a tap dance on that high wire. With a Variable Annuity, you can have that safety net, and you can make those funds do a dance in a much more aggressive fashion than you might otherwise choose.

By the way, the words *stock market*, assumes you know that a VA account is a security, and is subject to all the rules and regulations pertaining to securities. This means that you will not only be presented with a lovely document called a prospectus, you will also have a raft of paperwork to fill out to satisfy the authorities that you are not totally daft for committing funds to a VA account.

# OBJECTIONS

In this chapter, we will review all the negatives you have heard about Variable Annuities, and it is hoped you will come to understand why all those people who have placed money in such accounts are not total idiots, as some would have you believe. Typically, these objections are as follows:

- Fees are too high and are not necessary

- Surrender charges are not necessary

- Taxes are assessed at ordinary income rates

- Choices are too difficult to understand

There is no question that Variable Annuities can be complicated. They offer a range of options that many find confusing, along with fees that are charged to take advantage of them. While these are the fees that receive attention from the investment intelligentsia, these can also be called *peace of mind* fees.

No one would question the value of paying a fee to protect your home and possessions from loss by fire, tornado and other disasters. If it costs 1% to 2% of the value of your property to obtain that peace of mind, doesn't it make sense to pay a fee to know that your life savings can grow in the securities market without fearing loss of principal? Indeed, as we will see, with some VA's you can assure not only preservation of principal, you can guarantee that your principal will increase. Is that worth a fee to you?

This book is written in the belief that you will be better served to use your own full knowledge of the big picture rather than rely on the opinion of *experts*. It is much easier to become your own financial expert than your own medical expert. That is the whole idea of your taking your time to read these pages.

If you look at a typical VA, you will see a variety of investment alternatives made available to you. This is similar to looking at a family of mutual funds that offer 20 to 100 different portfolio alternatives ranging from conservative to aggressive.

The VA, however, will typically offer the same range of investment alternatives from various management companies selected by the insurance company, and from the whole universe of funds. What you see is the result of their scrutiny of the entire marketplace and their decision of which money managers to utilize in order to make their company attractive to you as an investor. Allowing them to select from over 8,000 funds makes your job easier. Even with the advantage of their selection process on your side, you still must make some choices.

The problem of *over-choice* can be handled quite nicely by simply asking the company to set up an asset allocation model tailored to your risk profile. And then, if you so instruct, they will automatically re-allocate funds at such regular intervals as you request to maintain the percentage allocation among the various investment choices you originally made. Because this rebalancing is done inside the annuity account, it is not a taxable transaction, and you need not be concerned with accounting for any gain or loss on the exchange.

This speaks to another significant difference between mutual fund investing and using the same fund managers inside a Variable Annuity.

Let's say that you have realized a substantial gain in your mutual fund account, as many did prior to 2001, and, you are becoming concerned to such an extent that you think it would be advisable to sell your mutual fund and move into a more conservative alternative.

With a mutual fund family, you need to consider the tax impact of switching funds, and may elect to ride it out to avoid paying taxes on your gains. With the VA, tax impact has no bearing on your decision, because switching funds will not be taxable. There are many mutual fund holders who rode the stock market down after 2001 and have yet to get back to where their accounts peaked.

This is a tax advantage the "experts" never seem to mention. It works the same as in a Qualified Plan such as an IRA account. Mutual fund investors outside of qualified plans can enjoy fund exchanges, but not without the need to account for taxable gain or loss.

While all Variable Annuities can be regarded as conservative investment vehicles, there are some folks who like to outguess the experts by timing the market. Here is where non-taxable fund switching gets very interesting, even though this practice is not encouraged by the insurance companies. In fact, there are several companies that offer an array of sector funds for those who think they can ride the wave of the most promising industries. (*When it comes to financial forecasters, you are fortunate if you find one who is more reliable than the local astrologer.*)

While talking taxes, let us address the main objection that we hear from the "experts"—the ultimate taxation at *ordinary* tax rates rather than capital gains rates. This certainly has credence on the face of it, but you never hear mention of it as an objection to putting money into and IRA or 401k plan. Money coming out of an IRA will be taxed at ordinary rates, and there comes a time when the IRS demands you withdraw money even if you do not need it. With an annuity, you can control when you decide to make a withdrawal, and can defer it as long as you want.

The tax illustration you will see used by the objectors makes the assumption that the account is fully liquidated and compares the tax results of such a total liquidation. The real world does not work that way. Annuities typically are liquidated gradually, in accordance with the whole idea of annuitization. Or, they pass to a beneficiary who then gets the tax bill, along with a number of options to control the tax impact.

There is a study made by recognized national accounting firm regarding the taxation question if full liquidation is the selection of the account holder (*taxicide*). The results are that the annuity comes out ahead on a long term basis, even when full liquidation is utilized. A similar study available from an economics professor concludes the same, and the tax deferral example in the appendix also holds true.

There is no need to mention tax advantages to any mutual fund investor who has been confronted with a 1099 form for capital gains for the same year they saw the value of their account go down. There are many such investors out there. The same funds held in a VA account would also go down with the market, but at least you would not be saddled with a capital gains tax bill to add salt to the wound. By the same token, capital losses in a VA account do not count on your tax return. If you like to have the ability to report such losses for a tax credit, you might wish to stick with the mutual funds.

There is another tax-related question that often comes up. It centers around the idea of using any form of an annuity inside a tax sheltered 401k or IRA account. The argument: 'It does not make sense to place a tax shelter inside a tax shelter.' That sounds reasonable, right?

However, no annuity charges for sheltering taxes—the shelter is provided by the laws of the land. In other words, taxes are *not* part of the decision. To hold to the premise that you should never put annuities in an IRA or 401K account totally disregards any other advantage that annuities offer, particularly as to preservation of your money.

The real question is: FEES. So, if you hear the tax shelter inside a tax shelter argument, you can disregard anything else that source has to say. Fees are another matter!

## FEES, FEES AND MORE FEES

The experts of the world love to sing the song of high fees. A recent writer in a major metropolitan newspaper cautioned employees considering a buyout from a major manufacturing firm to avoid any salesperson offering annuities of any sort, saying they have high fees and are too complicated. But, there was no alternative mentioned that was any better. It is as if the salesperson is laying in wait for you to buy their plan so they can pay their bills.

It is easy for the benefits of annuities to be dismissed as 'pricey gimmicks', and you seldom hear any mention of 'benefits' those fees provide. Many in the media who criticize annuities get paid a fee for their opinions, and that is fine. The alternative investments they recommend are not free of fees. And—you never hear an expert mention the fact that stocks have sales charges, and ALL mutual funds have fees, including charges to get in, charges to get out, and many with added charges while you are in (12b-1 fees). There is no such thing as a free lunch. Who do you think is paying the fund manager, advertising, etc., etc.? Not to mention…

# TAXES ARE A FEE!

If you check with any of the companies that are the recognized authorities on mutual funds, you will find that the average reduction of your return from the assessment of income taxes exceeds 2%. Now, if you reduce your overall return 2% to pay taxes, or by the same amount to provide benefits to yourself that add to your peace of mind, which would you choose?

If you are the type of person who visualizes the waiter in a restaurant looking to load you up with the most expensive entrée on the menu, you probably need to look at another financial menu. If you are more interested in how the recommendation suits your appetite, then you might look at exactly how the VA investment menu suits your financial appetite. Some of the offerings you will find are simply not available with other investment forms.

Speaking of restaurants and such, the fee common to all VA accounts is something called an M & E fee. No—it does not stand for meals and entertainment! It is for a Mortality and Expense charge, and typically costs about 1.4% of the account value. The expense part is understandable. Even a bank CD includes an expense fee—you just do not see it! The mortality charge should be explained.

Part of the mortality fee helps to offset a death penalty cost to heirs. This would come into play if at the time of the death of the account holder, the value of the account had been trashed in the marketplace. Let us say that for every dollar originally invested, the account value at death had fallen to 50 cents. In such a case the insurance company would bring the account value back to $1.00 to the heirs. In the market slide after 2001, this benefit paid out close to $3,000,000 to heirs from the last figures we have seen.

Until recently, we have not seen any annuity that allowed a client to eliminate the fee for Mortality expense—probably a foolish choice in any event. Why would you choose to let your heirs pay the penalty if it turns out that you made lousy investment choices? But if you are phobic about fees, here is an opportunity for you to investigate.

While thinking about it, the subject of fees should include the fact that the manager of each investment alternative, called sub-accounts, charges a fee, and it is stated in the prospectus in a manner that allows you to compare, if you wish. Further comment here is of no value, since those same managers charge a fee for managing the funds wherever they are. They should be comparable, but it is easy to research if you have a mind to.

If you are not fee-phobic, there is an added fee you can pay that agrees to not only reimburse your heirs for your original deposit, it will return the investment as if it had compounded at the rate of 5% per year. Would you be a bit more aggressive in your investment decisions if you had this assurance? We would hope so. It is called an 'enhanced death benefit' and the cost to have it is somewhere in the neighborhood of 1/2 of 1% of the account value. If the funds you are investing are intended for your heirs, the availability of this benefit makes it seem almost foolish not to be more aggressive in your investment choices. It is now possible to guarantee that your account value at death will be reset each year to the highest prior anniversary account value. Is that worth a fee to anybody?

What we have just discussed is called a *death benefit* guarantee. However, most people are more interested in benefits available during their own lifetime, with benefits to heirs being of lesser interest.

Case in point: Let us say that you are ten years away from retirement and will need your IRA funds then to supply income for your retirement. If your investment advisor charges you 5% to manage your account in the stock market, but guarantees that your account will double in ten years even after payment of his fee, would you sign up with him? What if he charges 10% and offers the same guarantee? If the answer is YES, then you recognize that it is not the fee that is paramount, it is the result. (By the way, it is illegal for any advisor to make such a guarantee!)

Here is some news for you: You can get that guarantee with a Variable Annuity for a lot less than 5%! The guarantee will be in writing and it will be backed up by a major financial institution whose financial substance can be known to you in advance. You can do this with that much maligned financial tool called a 'Variable Annuity'.

Annuity accounts may actually be looked to for income someday, so it is significant to eliminate guesswork, right? This is where you will incur some added fees, so let us now look to the menu for:

# LIVING BENEFIT GUARANTEES !

Here goes! Let us try to give you as current a picture of the options available in spite of the fact that we continue to see innovations come forth that boggle the mind of even the most experienced advisor. This is where it helps to have someone you trust hold your hand. If that person is able to listen to your needs, and has access to a variety of companies to meet those needs, you should throw your arms around him or her and not let go.

# GUARANTEED MINIMUM WITHDRAWAL BENEFIT

Many companies now offer something called a Guaranteed Minimum Withdrawal benefit. One that we know of makes a charge of .35% of the account value (a little more than 1/3rd of 1%) to guarantee that you can take an income from the money right away and be assured that you will get all your money back in spite of what the stock market does, as long as you do not exceed 7% withdrawals per year.

In a worst case situation, the account will pay out fully in just over 14 years. If the stock market is nice to you, you can periodically update this guarantee, and at the same time increase your income. (We *know of an account set up that has been receiving 7% withdrawals for several years now, and the account value has still increased over 25%. The client can increase the withdrawals in a couple of years, even if the account stops growing.)*

There is an alternative to this plan from mutual funds, and it is also called a withdrawal plan. If you take a 7% annual income, you may or may not have it last 14 years, depending on what the stock market does. With the annuity charge mentioned above, there is no question you will receive your money back.

# GUARANTEED ACCOUNT VALUE

Then comes along a benefit called a Guaranteed Account Value benefit. One company simply describes this as "The worst you can do is the best you have done!" It simply provides you with a living benefit that allows you to invest in the market without putting your principal at risk—if you have the willingness to wait for the 5th anniversary to have the guarantee honored.

This benefit can escalate after the 5th anniversary. On each anniversary date after the 5th, the company looks back to the value five years prior, and you are guaranteed that this value will be your new principal guarantee. Prior gains are locked in automatically. The value of this feature is designed to appeal to those with a longer term outlook and a desire to be more aggressive investors than they would be without the guarantee.

Obviously, many people who have money in IRA accounts have that longer term perspective, and this option can allow them to open up their choices to a more growth oriented investment menu. Since the insurance company is a watchful partner in this program, they are not going to allow you to go overboard in your choices. (*Perhaps this would be a good plan to offer to those wishing to control their Social Security future with private accounts! No more worry about the stock market 'casino'!*)

## 5% INCOME FOR LIFE??

Now there is a benefit for income oriented investors who would like to have income but do not want to annuitize. It is a lifetime income provision that lets you take withdrawals for AS LONG AS YOU LIVE and still have access to your principal.

For example, if you have a made a $100,000 deposit, you can be assured of an income of $5,000 every year for as long as you live. Even if the investment accounts become depleted—the income will be there. That is what the contract guarantees. One company that does this makes a charge of 6/10th of one percent of the account value for this feature.

On the other hand, you can work this benefit to increase your income after a few years if your investment accounts do well. With the safety net of this contractual guarantee, you can now comfortably become a more aggressive investor than you would otherwise be. Let the guarantor, the insurance company, watch over the account so that your life can thus be made free from worry about the direction of the stock market.

## GUARANTEED MINIMUM INCOME BENEFIT

Much of financial planning has to do with solving the problem of retirement—how to establish enough savings to live a comfortable life in the retirement years. Wouldn't it be nice to know for certain that your savings would be there to guarantee income for as long as you live, regardless of how the economy or the stock market performs? And wouldn't it be nice to know that you would participate in the stock market if it did well? Would you be inclined to be more growth oriented in your investment selections?

The guaranteed minimum income benefit (GMIB) is intended to allow you to know what your income will be when you need it in future years. And because it is in an annuity account, you will have all the payout options that only are available with insurance contracts. Most importantly, you know that there will always be a check coming to you for your lifetime. Today, it is possible to know that your money will earn a minimum of 7% over ten years, even if the stock market goes nowhere. That will be the capital base for your retirement account. You may do better than that—but not less. That is the contractual guarantee.

Some advisors will tell you that this is no big deal, and that you can do the same on your own without paying a fee. It is appropriate to ask these advisors if they will back up the guarantee with a contract from a major financial institution.

Variable Annuities have achieved ever increasing acceptance in the marketplace despite all the criticism leveled at them. This gives evidence that that there must be some substance to the benefits they offer. We continue to see more innovations in these benefits. While they may not be suitable for every investor, certainly for those open to the idea of considering them, there are multiple rewards available.

# CHAPTER 5

# THE SUPER ANNUITY

everal years ago, at a money show in Florida, there was a presentation made to over two hundred investors, mostly seniors. The title of the presentation was:

HOW TO DO YOUR STOCK MARKET

INVESTING AND PAY

NO TAXES ON DIVIDENDS

NO TAXES ON LONG TERM GAINS

NO TAXES ON EXCHANGES

AND

NO TAXES EVER!!

The presentation naturally was of interest to the group, but there was a noticeable slump when the mention was made of the "I" word (Life Insurance). While all the stated goals could be accomplished, it would be necessary to do so inside the confines of a Life Insurance policy. The response was reminiscent of the admonishment in the Bible to the rich man. To obtain the kingdom of heaven, he would have to abandon his wealth. As you may recall, he walked away in disappointment.

The aversion to any consideration of Life Insurance is quite common. Sometimes it can be attributed to a mindset that does not allow any contemplation of one's mortality. Or, it could be simply a result of prior training about the use of insurance with the idea that the need diminishes as you grow older. Whatever the reason, you will definitely benefit by taking another look, and by paying attention to some of the ideas presented in the following pages.

The same idea was presented in another way by a newspaper ad in a Florida Sunday paper some time ago, inviting people to attend seminars. The ad was quite attention getting. It read:

WHY THE IRS LOVES ANNUITIES!

(ALSO IRA'S AND 401K'S)

The seminars were filled, and the theme of his presentation was centered around this idea:

IF TAX DEFERRAL IS GOOD,

ISN'T TAX-FREE BETTER?

The claims made in these seminars describe the effect of combining an annuity with a small amount of Life Insurance. By including a sufficient amount of insurance, the tax complexion of the annuity is changed drastically. The objection of leaving behind a tax bill to your estate is eliminated. Now the account is paid out to the heirs as an insurance benefit, and not only are the proceeds tax free, the insurance benefit actually increases the total amount available to the heirs. This is what is known by some as a 'super annuity'.

If you choose to make a single deposit to an annuity account, it will grow with no taxes due until funds are withdrawn, either by you or your beneficiaries. If you deposit those same funds into a single payment Life Insurance contract, you still pay tax if you use the money during your lifetime. However, if the funds go to your beneficiary, they go to them tax free as Life Insurance proceeds. In addition, the beneficiary receives the increased amount from the insurance.

Somewhere in this chapter, it will be necessary to talk about a MEC, which stands for a:

# MODIFIED ENDOWMENT CONTRACT

That fancy term came into effect as a result of a law passed in 1988 known as TAMRA (Technical and Miscellaneous Revenue Act). The effect of it was to correct what was seen to be an abuse of the single deposit Life Insurance plan. Investors were using it as a tax favored bank account, and with the high interest rates being credited at the time, it was quite popular. You could make withdrawals from your account as taking back your principal and not be taxed on them until you had totally withdrawn your original deposit. Under the new law, your withdrawals are considered to be withdrawals of interest first and only from your invested principal after all interest earnings have been withdrawn.

Annuities are also taxed on this basis, which is referred to as LIFO (last in, first out). The last money credited to the account is the first money withdrawn. The exception to this rule is when you elect one of the payout options. If you elect a payout option, each payment is taxed partly as interest, and partly as return of principal in accordance with a mathematically calculated formula.

With the single deposit Life Insurance plan, your lifetime withdrawals are subject to the same tax treatment as annuities. The difference is in the tax treatment of the beneficiaries. You can look upon single payment life as an 'heir conditioned' annuity. The proceeds are treated as Life Insurance benefits. As such they are not only increased by the insurance benefit, but they are not subject to any income tax. This arrangement provides a ready solution to those who criticize the ultimate taxability of annuity accounts by providing

# A TAX FREE ACCOUNT TO THE HEIRS!

Most annuity owners are oblivious to the fact that their annuities are not tax forgiveness tools. While they may be great for having values build up over the years, someday the taxes will become due. If not paid during their lifetime, then the tax bill will go to the beneficiaries. At that time, it will become too late to avoid including the tax collector as a beneficiary.

If you put $100,000 into annuity contracts, and it grows to $200,000 over the years, there is a profit of $100,000 that has not been taxed. If you take the money out during your life, you will pay taxes on the gain. If you leave the annuity to your heirs, they will get the tax bill. The probability is that they will pay tax on the $100,000 profit at the highest bracket out there at the time they receive the funds.

If you think this is bad, consider this: The same $100,000 put in an IRA account over the years is <u>fully taxable</u>. The tax collector loves this even more than annuities. The IRS merely needs to patiently wait for the value of the account to build. The longer it builds, the bigger the ultimate tax will be, and that is why the ad says that the IRS loves IRA accounts. Whoopee! At least with an annuity, during your lifetime you can control when the tax bill comes due. And, if you liquidate the account entirely, your originally invested principal is not taxable.

Is there a way to beat the tax collector? The answer to this is yes— partially. The reason for only partial relief is that any gains already realized in the annuity must be taxable any time they are moved outside the annuity. This leads us to a discussion of another way to use annuities, called a

# NON MODIFIED ENDOWMENT

It is possible to amend the tax situation on a MEC by paying attention to the guidelines set up under TAMRA. These are guidelines to limit the amount of money invested as a single deposit, or as a deposit over the first 7 years. Making premium deposits in excess of the guideline limit results in the account being classified as a MEC.

If you want to have full tax free access to your Life Insurance plan, you may wish to consider using an annuity for your single deposit, and have the company make payments over 7 years from the annuity to the Life Insurance plan, thus complying with the '7-pay limit'. Taxes are due only on the interest earned by the annuity during that period.

The end result of this will be a non-modified endowment plan. No longer will you be subject to taxes on withdrawals of the interest earnings on the insurance account. Most insurance companies are set up to decline premiums that would exceed the guidelines and turn the account into a MEC.

Your next comment is likely to be: I already have enough Life Insurance—right? If this is your situation, why not find someone in the family who could use more insurance, and offer to provide a benefit to them with no cash outlay. You can still own the account and control its use during your lifetime. Do you have a child or grandchild who could use more insurance? I will give an example of how this can work in a following chapter.

Yes, there is a cost to having the Life Insurance benefit, but there is a cost to NOT having it, and that cost is called INCOME TAX. If the money in the annuity is intended to go to your estate, a competent agent will help you make a cost comparison. You can expect to find the cost of the insurance benefit to be substantially less than the tax costs that will ultimately occur. Why not have those tax dollars work to the benefit of someone you care for?

Traditionally, people are trained to think of Life Insurance as protection against early death, and of annuities as a way to protect against living too long. A *super annuity*, then, is actually a Life Insurance policy with an accent on the build-up of value of the cash accumulation account. In that respect, it resembles an annuity and it combines answers to both living needs, and estate transfer needs. Many informed people are using this account as a financial tool to accomplish the same things you would do with annuities, but with even greater tax efficiency.

So, then you ask; "Well, Mr. Smart Guy, that sounds pretty good, but if I switch my annuity over to a Life Insurance account, I not only need to pay the tax on the earnings already made, but I also have to pay a surrender charge to get the money from my present annuity company. How do I avoid that charge?" Tune in later to the chapter— "A*ctivate that Annuity,"* and you will find an example of how you can avoid the surrender charge and stop the tax drain for your heirs.

# BUY TERM AND INVEST THE DIFFERENCE

No doubt you have heard the advice that the only thing Life Insurance companies are to be used for is to provide the cheapest form of protection available—Term Insurance. To put *savings* money into an insurance contract is a mistake, it is claimed, as these funds can be better invested elsewhere. The assumption is that your savings receive shabby treatment in an insurance policy.

This line of reasoning goes back to the days when agents told you to save for retirement with Life Insurance and were never able to tell you what interest rate you would receive on your savings. If they knew what the rate was, they would not tell you because it was so low.

Nowadays, however, the insurance agent need not shy away from a discussion of interest rates. With the advent of 'current interest' forms of insurance, you can now assess the merit of using Life Insurance as a savings vehicle. With variable life contracts, you can also invest in the stock market through the various sub-accounts offered. In other words, you can exercise control over your investments, and do so in a tax favored environment.

Per the rules controlling MEC's as previously discussed, it is possible to design an insurance plan that minimizes the insurance element and maximizes the investment portion. By doing so you can actually make the account look more like an investment account similar to an IRA or Roth IRA but without the restrictions.

Modern insurance contracts also allow you to have the insurance company pay the beneficiary the account value *in addition* to the face amount insurance benefit. This eliminates the problem once voiced that, 'the insurance company stole my cash value'.

You can now see exactly what you are paying for the insurance element of you policy, and you will also find the costs to be quite competitive with the costs of term insurance purchased separately. In addition, it allows you to have the insurance paid with *pre-tax* dollars rather than *after-tax* dollars. This is a significant advantage that deserves further comment.

> If you go to the marketplace to buy a loaf of bread or *Term Life Insurance*, the dollars you use are the dollars that have already been taxed. In order to spend a dollar, you will need to earn something more than that dollar, pay the tax on it and then spend it.

> If you put the same dollars into a savings plan with Life Insurance, you will be using dollars that have already been taxed—the same as a Roth IRA. With the insurance plan, however, you can have Life Insurance included for which there is a premium charged to the account. Since the earnings in the account are sheltered from taxes, part of the cost of the insurance protection will be offset by the tax savings on those earnings. That is what is meant by using *pre-tax* dollars.

One wonders if those advocating exclusive use of term insurance would also advise you to always rent your home, rather than buy it. If you have an ongoing need for shelter, could it not be maintained that there is an on going need or desire for Life Insurance protection? Indeed, the term insurance buyer will one day have to confront the problem of looking at a large premium increase if continued coverage is desired.

It is popular in some quarters to criticize insurance policies as investment vehicles. Yet, for the open minded investor, there are some substantial advantages to such plans. Indeed, as illustrated in chapter 8, some of the potential investment characteristics are so incomparable that they almost defy credibility—they sound 'too good to be true'.

# Chapter 6

# MAKING ANNUITIES PAY

As more and more Americans find that traditional pension plans are being replaced in favor of 401K plans, there likely will be a growing interest in becoming knowledgeable about the benefits of annuities. With increasing longevity an ongoing fact, the need to be aware of choices that guarantee a lifetime income to function as a pension will become more obvious.

Since this is the avowed purpose of annuities in the first place, a separate chapter is in order. Isn't it interesting that payout options are seldom mentioned in the annuity discussions that you listen to? While a guaranteed income is a wonderful and unique benefit, evidence indicates that most annuities are never *annuitized*. With the changing pension environment, this can be expected to change.

Funds parked in an annuity are boring! They are about as exciting as watching paint dry. They just sit there and grow as time passes. Not that there is anything wrong or boring about such growth! It is just the fact that these funds are capable of providing much more action, and we will elaborate on this in the following chapter.

Annuities are intended to produce an income. In fact, they are the only way to guarantee that there will not be too much life left over at the end of the money. They are a contractual guarantee of a periodic income for as long as you live!

As previously stated, if you set up an annuity account to start paying you a regular check from the beginning, you have what is called an immediate annuity. This is also referred to as the *payout stage*. If you do not want to have the income to start right away, you have what is called a deferred annuity—the funds accumulate in the account to be used later—otherwise known as the 'accumulation' stage.

## IMMEDIATE ANNUITIES

Look upon this alternative as a "do it yourself" pension plan. It works this way: You agree with the insurance company to turn a lump sum amount into a guaranteed lifetime monthly payout or a payout for a specified period of time. Once you make that agreement, both you and the insurance company are locked into the agreement. With some exceptions, you lose access to your deposit. That is the reason many choose not to use an immediate annuity.

You may recall that the sales person told you that you would be given choices when the time came to get your money back. Broadly speaking, you can break down the choices into two categories:

1.  Lifetime income
2.  Non Lifetime income

Some form of lifetime income is the most appropriate choice for most people. The benefit is to have the income stream guaranteed for life, like a pension. That is the thing that makes insurance companies different from other financial alternatives.

When you see the word *lifetime*, you know that you will be involved with mortality tables, and your check will be affected by a number of factors, including your age and gender. In some cases, your health will be a factor also, as there are some companies that will increase your payout if your health is poor. They figure they will not need to payout as long a period of time.

Since people are living longer, it makes sense to lock in annuity rates based on current mortality tables, as the future payouts will need to be calculated on a longer expected lifespan.

You should be aware that, while the lifetime payout is a contract that the insurance company must honor, the amount of your payout check is subject to the risk of inflation. A fixed income loses purchasing power in an inflationary economy. (Would you accept a pension with no cost of living adjustment?) This is certainly an important factor when you are electing lifetime payout options.

One way to deal with the inflation risk is to find a company that offers a payout that increases as time goes by. Another is to use a Variable Annuity, where the payout will be affected by variance in the investment performance of your sub-account selections. Some are available that specify a minimum income that acts as a floor in case the securities accounts perform poorly.

If the idea of a Variable Annuity is repugnant to you, the good news is that at least one company has a 'fixed' annuity that allows for increased income geared to the performance of a stock market index. You can set this up and know that your check can increase but will never be less than 90% of your initial income check.

Here are some of the lifetime payout plans you can expect:

Life Only: Payment is for your own life duration and stops when you die. Nothing is left behind for the heirs. This is the perfect plan for the person who says the goal is to have the money be totally used up on the date of death, but wants to make sure the income will last even if he lives to the age of 157.

Joint and Survivor payout: Here the income stream is based on two lives, and will continue to be paid until the survivor passes. You can elect to have the check remain the same for both lives, or to be set up at one level while both parties live, and a lower level to the survivor.

Life with Period Certain: Under this arrangement, the income is guaranteed to last a minimum number of years, (5, 10, 15 or 20) even if the recipient passes on. In that event the payments continue to a named beneficiary until the guarantee period is completed.

Payments for a Certain Period: This does not involve a mortality factor, since income is spread out over a set number of years (generally 5 or 10 years). This is an example of a non-lifetime annuity. The obligation is similar to a bank account paying out over the same period. This is not the option most people would choose unless they are seeking to move money out of an annuity in such a way as to avoid a surrender charge. (See the chapter on *Super Annuities and the example in the following chapter!*) It can also be utilized as a way to move money into a 'super annuity' plan to set up a 'non-modified endowment'. A variation of the 'period certain' option is called a 'refund' option where the income continues until all the account is used up.

# ANNUITIZATION

We have previously mentioned the word *annuitization*. That is a nasty word for some people for the simple reason that it is commonly understood to mean that you must give up control of your money. But, as the song says: "It ain't necessarily so!"

In the first place, there are companies that will allow you to change your mind, and they will return the 'commuted' value to you. How they calculate this is not important, as there are better ways to go about it if you want an income without giving up control of your money.

One of these ways is to establish a **'systematic withdrawal'** plan which is similar to making a regular withdrawal from your bank account. Like the bank account, there is no guarantee that your money will not run out during your lifetime.

Now comes a new alternative from the Variable Annuity community. They will give you a lifetime income stream of 5% and will guarantee that you will always have a check in your mailbox as long as you live—and you will always have access to your money if you want to take it. Even better, they will offer you a chance to increase your check (and your guarantee), if your account value manages to increase over time. This is basically a systematic withdrawal plan backed up by a contractually guaranteed income for life. This is a pretty neat plan—an income that goes the distance without killing the craving for liquidity.

## WHAT IS A SPLIT ANNUITY?

Probably more people have heard of a banana split than have heard of a Split Annuity. But for those folks who are looking for their nest egg to produce a check in the mail every month, this alternative is well worth knowing about. Not only will it solve the problem of annuitization, it can be designed by a competent professional to provide for future income increases.

A Split Annuity is actually two annuities. One is used to provide that monthly check, and it is intended to be used up entirely over a period of 5 to 10 years, using the Payments for a Period Certain option referred to earlier in this chapter. The other annuity is intended to grow over that income period in an amount sufficient to bring the investment balance back to the original amount invested, at which time the whole process can be repeated.

In the initial income period, the income is largely free of taxation for the simple reason that it is merely a return of your investment. You are taxed only on the interest the account earns. In reality, you could do this with a bank or other investment if you can find a higher yield than the insurance company is using. There is really no mortality consideration involved as there would be when a 'lifetime' payout is selected.

The amount of income you receive in the initial period is calculated by the amount you need to put in the replacement annuity, and that is determined by whatever interest rate you assume it will earn over that period. It is possible these days to use a Variable Annuity that guarantees 7% over 10 years, but allows it to do better if there are favorable results from the investments you select. This would allow you to receive a higher level of income when you start the next cycle, and thus act as an offset to inflation.

Consider this: If you have a long term time frame, this 7% guarantee will mean that income base will basically double in 10 years. Thus, you can design an income for the first 10 years using about one-half of your funds, and let the other half double over ten years to fully replace your original principal.

Currently this would allow you to receive an income over 6% on a guaranteed basis, and over 80 percent would be non taxable. In 10 years, your income base would be at least returned in full, and possibly increased with the value of the investments in the account.

There is an alternative available from mutual funds. It is called the monthly withdrawal plan, and it sets up an income based on a withdrawal level you select—typically 6% or 7%. This does not carry the same guarantee as the annuity, and for those who are not willing to trust the vagaries of the stock market, why chance it? If you can participate in the stock market with a 7% guarantee that you will get back all your money at the very least, why gamble?

Why not use annuities as soon as possible to generate regular income? If the income is not needed to pay for grocery bills or mortgage payments, there are a number of reasons to take income in the following chapter. The chapter comments more extensively on the use of payout alternatives, and how to make that annuity account perform to maximize your financial goals.

# Chapter 7

# ACTIVATE THAT ANNUITY!

As mentioned in the previous chapter, most annuities are never converted to an income stream. Rather, they are held as financial reserves for unforeseen contingencies, then they are passed on to the heirs when not utilized during the lifetime of the owner. If you view your present annuities in this way, you might wish to consider re-evaluation with some of the ideas we will present here. Annuities are great funding vehicles for many needs beyond buying groceries and paying for electric bills.

It is interesting to observe how many of the senior citizens who reach the age of 70 1/2 and are required to start taking money from their IRA and 401k accounts object to being forced to take the money. They do not like having to pay the income taxes because they really are not in need of the money. (One of the advantages of *non-qualified* annuities is that there is no such mandatory withdrawal.)

You might ask yourself at one point in your planning process the following question about your finances:

**What kind of money is this? Is it intended to provide primarily for my own living needs? Or is it money to be a part of my legacy?**

Your response to these questions will determine what your planner will recommend for your consideration. Be forewarned that some of these recommendations may involve taking the step of paying a tax bill on your IRA or annuity holding ahead of time. There is nothing illegal or unwise about doing so. It just goes against the ingrained idea that you must incur a tax bill to do so, and you have been trained to put off paying a tax bill until it is absolutely unavoidable.

If you are committed to the program of delaying taxes, you may wish to reassess for several reasons. First, the taxes will likely be larger in the future if you wait to pay them. Secondly, for the small cost of taxes incurred now, you will establish a far superior financial plan to enhance your welfare while you are living, or the amount you leave behind at death.

It is very easy to put off making financial decisions, and procrastination comes easy. Sometimes, however, circumstances occur that serve as a reminder that the time has come to bite the bullet and get serious about getting organized financially. The following story is an example.

Some years ago, there was a lady who was a widow and was distressed by the large income tax bill she was forced to pay every year. That bill, presented to her by her accountant, usually exceeded $16,000.

She had adequate income to live quite well without needing the interest generated from her CD's that were presenting her with 1099 forms every year. The accountant dutifully recorded the interest when preparing her return, and he gave her the news of how much her taxes were for the year. With the erosion of the bank interest by taxes, plus inflation, she was obviously a viable candidate to take advantage of annuities. She was totally unfamiliar with annuities.

The advice given to her was simply to move the money she had in bank accounts over into annuities. Some of her money could not be moved as it was from a private source that resulted from a business sale. The remainder could be moved, however, and doing so resulted in not only a larger interest credit for her money, but also in sheltering that income from current taxation. The bottom line was that her tax bill from that point on never exceeded $5,000. Over the years, in taxes alone, her trust in her adviser resulted in over $100,000 in tax savings.

Some critics would say that she was subjected to surrender charges if she needed to make a withdrawal, and that is true. However, the charges vanished over a few years time, and she always had access to 10% of her accounts each year with no penalty. Had she continued with her bank accounts, she would have had a penalty to pay with each rollover if she needed the money in addition to the larger penalty of a much higher income tax bill.

Other critics would point out that she merely put off the tax bill to a later time, and that her heirs would likely get that bill. That also is true. However, it did not come to pass in her case because some of the tax savings were used to obtain sufficient Life Insurance to pay the deferred taxes. In fact, she was able to afford a lot more insurance by simply using just a portion of the annual tax savings. The bottom line is that the heirs were better off by close to a quarter of a million dollars, her tax returns were done at no cost and her advisor was well compensated for his efforts, and...

## SHE NEVER PAID A FEE!

While the heirs never expressed appreciation for what was done for them, the advisor was gratified by the trust this lady placed in him. She would simply put all mail that looked like annuity information or insurance into a safe place, and wait for him to come around to throw out what was not needed. The achievement of that level of trust is what every planner savors. It is the frosting on the cake that cannot be measured in terms of dollars.

The above example is a classic solution to the use of the tax management capabilities of annuities. In the remainder of this chapter, we will present some further examples that may be appropriate solutions for any reader to utilize.

# A GOOD INVESTMENT???

SITUATION: A potential client was the beneficiary of a sum of money that enabled he and his wife to live well with no concerns about money. Having no children or family, they had expressed an interest in establishing a charitable fund to leave behind. Through actual experience, they had been made aware of the ability of the stock market to lose principal, and wanted to avoid such losses in the future.

SOLUTION: Client was told that he could to turn $100,000 into a $500,000 legacy, and do so on <u>fully guaranteed </u>basis.

Here is what was proposed: Place the $100,000 into an annuity account that contractually guaranteed a 5% income for as long as they lived. It could be more if the investment accounts did well, but it could never be less. The income each year would be used to pay for a Life Insurance policy. Since they were both under the age of 60, and the policy paid off only on the passing of the surviving spouse, it was possible to have a face amount of $500,000. The premium was guaranteed to remain the same until they were 120 years old, so they never had to worry about surprise premium increases.

RESULTS:

- The client never had to worry about paying the insurance premiums

- He had a fully guaranteed way to create a substantial legacy for a favorite charity.

- He could take a deduction for the $5,000 premium from his current income tax if he so elected.

- He could change his mind at any time, and take the money out of his annuity account, and stop the entire program without penalty.

COMMENT: Here is a question for you: Do you know of any investment where you can turn a $100,000 investment into $500,000? *Guaranteed? Tax Free?* If not, you may wish to consider this idea for your favorite charity. That favorite charity, by the way, could be your own children or grandchildren.

# HOW TO PAY THE TAX BILL ON YOUR IRA!

SITUATION: Client had a substantial IRA account and was at an age where the IRS required a distribution each year, even if the money was not needed for income. Client was awakened to the tax bill the children would be faced with. Potentially, the IRS was the major beneficiary of the account.

SOLUTION: An annuity was set up to guarantee a payout of 7% with the ability to increase if the investment accounts performed well. Even if the stock market collapsed, the client would be assured that the money invested would be returned in full in a little over 14 years. The amount transferred was $150,000 and the 7% income produced enough to pay for $500,000 insurance for the client.

RESULTS:

- The insurance proceeds were a tax free account to the heirs

- They would be available to offset any taxes at death of the client on any remaining balance in the IRA account.

- Any amount not needed for paying taxes could be added to the heirs' educational funds for the grandchildren.

COMMENT: As it happened, the investment accounts have increased. Even after taking the 7% payout for a couple of years, the $150,000 deposit has grown by over 25%. On the 5th anniversary, the client will have the opportunity to update the guarantee to the current anniversary value of the account. If it simply remains at the current level, the principal will have increased. With a change in health that has occurred since the insurance was issued, it is not likely the client will ever stop the program.

# WHY BOTHER WITH A LIVING TRUST?

SITUATION: Widow, age 76, attended a seminar talking about the ravages of the probate system, and promoting a living trust as a way to avoid probate. She had just sold her home, and was looking for a way to maximize her estate for her children.

SOLUTION: Since the only assets that were titled in her name were a car and other personal effects, plus bank accounts, she set up two annuities. One was to provide an income for all her current living needs, including the insurance premiums for her Long Term Care insurance, and the other was to be a financial reserve for contingencies.

RESULTS:

- Her beneficiaries were designated in the annuity accounts, and did not need to go through probate.

- She retained a bank account for current cash needs and designated a contingent owner on the forms the bank provided.

- She needed a will for just her automobile, and the personal effects she left to her children. It was still subject to probate but with a simplified process.

- She avoided the expense and complication of setting up a trust.

COMMENT: This is not to say that she should not work with a competent attorney to make sure all other legal considerations are wrapped up. It merely points out one of the features of insurance contracts—probate avoidance.

# WHY PAY FOR LONG TERM CARE INSURANCE?

SITUATION: Client had an IRA account worth about $75,000, and was not yet of an age that required a withdrawal. Client had no coverage for Long Term Care, and regarded the $75,000 as the answer for that problem.

SOLUTION: The IRA was transferred to an annuity that guaranteed a 5% income for as long as the client lived, and the income was used to pay for a Life Insurance plan in the amount of $125,000. The plan was one that allowed the client to use up to 2% of the face amount if needed for health care during her lifetime. Whatever portion of the face amount that was not needed for health care, that amount would be passed as a tax free life insurance benefit to the heirs.

RESULTS:

- Client has increased the total amount available for Long Term Care costs from $75,000 to $200,000, assuming at least a 5% return on the annuity.

- Client has no concern about coming up with money to pay insurance premiums in the future.

- Client has increased coverage for Long Term Care that pays even if care is not needed!

- Client retained the ability to quit and use the principal for other things.

COMMENT: You can expect to see more and more Life Insurance plans made available that allow an 'accelerated' benefit when the need for Long Term Care arises. What this means is that you do not need to die in order to use the insurance. Normally, with such plans, you can access up to 2% of the face amount each month to pay for care, either at home or in a facility. Typically, if you have the ability to set aside just the cost of a one year stay in a facility, you can make that one year deposit last for three years if you are insurable and willing to take advantage of the leveraging power of insurance.

# CHANGING FROM TAX DEFERRED TO 'TAX FREE'

SITUATION: Client had an annuity that was purchased over one year ago, but still had a surrender charge. The current account value was $110,000. To liquidate the account immediately would incur that charge, but it could be avoided by taking an income spread out over 5 years or more. Since the annuity was likely to be passed along to the children anyway, and the client had been made aware of the 'tax free' benefits of insurance to the beneficiary, the client wanted to take advantage of the more tax efficient insurance plan

SOLUTION: The annuity was set up to provide an annual income over a 10 year period. There would be a monthly payout of $1,068 which at age 68 was sufficient to purchase in full a $250,000 face amount of insurance protection. The form of policy purchased provided that up to 2% of the face amount would be available if needed for Long Term Care.

RESULTS:

- Instead of a $110,000 annuity with a growing tax liability, the client established an immediate $250,000 tax free legacy account for his heirs.

- The client avoided all surrender charges

- The client had access to $5,000 per month of the insurance proceeds if needed for Long Term Care, either at home or in a nursing facility.

COMMENT: It is quite advantageous to be open to the power of a Life Insurance plan—even at an older age. This becomes more interesting with the increasing use of Life Insurance to pay for Long Term Care. Your good health is worth a lot of money!

# THE DOWNSIZED EXECUTIVE

SITUATION: A mid level executive for a large manufacturing firm was a victim of downsizing and was looking for employment. He had a large 401K account that he took with him, but wanted to work for another five years until he turned 65. He wanted his nest egg to grow as much as possible to provide him a check every month when he turned 65.

SOLUTION: Being aware of the potential for loss of principal as well as the potential for growth, he considered one of the mutual funds that offered a guarantee of principal, but he found their investment restrictions and fees to be unattractive. He decided to invest his 401K fund in a Variable Annuity that offered over 70 investment alternatives, and still guaranteed his account would grow by a minimum of 5% even if the market went south.

RESULTS:

- For not much more cost than the mutual fund alternative, he was able to take an aggressive approach in the stock market.

- He was also able to project his minimum income from his holdings when he needed them in 5 years.

- If the investment selections did well, his income would increase proportionately.

- He could elect to have a minimum 5% income check from his account in 5 years that was contractually guaranteed to last as long as he lived.

# THE DOTING GRANDPARENT

SITUATION: Grandparent had $50,000 that he wished to set aside for his two grand children's education. A friend had done so by putting money into an annuity at the bank.

SOLUTION: Rather than using an annuity, the agent suggested that he set up a single deposit, dividend paying Life Insurance. He was 70 years of age, and the $50,000 deposit would create an immediate tax free benefit of $74,000.

RESULTS:

- The education fund was immediately increased almost 50% by the amount of the insurance benefit.

- The deposit continued to grow with dividends, increasing the total insurance benefit as time went by.

- He retained access to the money if it was needed during his own lifetime

- The 10th year insurance benefit grew to nearly $87,000

- He left no income tax bill to his grandchildren.

# THE GIFTING ALTERNATIVE

SITUATION: A senior citizen wanted a way to make a gift of $11,000 each year in a way that would create the most value for his son's family.

SOLUTION: $11,000 deposit each year was made into a variable Universal Life plan that made the face amount whatever the 7 pay TAMRA limit would allow. At the son's age of 35, that amount was $295,000. The son was agreeable to letting the money grow as a fund for future educational expense or as a retirement supplement.

RESULTS:

- Assuming a deposit of $11,000 for 4 years, with a rate of return of 9% on the investment selections in the insurance account, there was an account worth $136,000 at the end of the 20th year.

- If not needed for education, and the fund was allowed to grow until the end of the 30th year, it was worth over $292,000.

- The Life Insurance remained in full force with no premiums required It actually increased in the later years to remain compliant with the tax laws.

- The account values were available at any time on a tax free basis, and that includes a tax free income as a retirement supplement.

NOTE: This illustration makes no mention of using an annuity. Rather, the gift is made directly to an insurance plan, recognizing that a planner must be open to listening to the goals of his client.

# INCREASING A CHARITABLE BEQUEST.

SITUATION: Client had made a decision in her will to leave money to her church. She would have given the money during her own lifetime, but wanted the money to be available if her health required her to go into a nursing home.

SOLUTION: She was able to move the money that was intended for the church into an annuity account that paid a higher rate of interest than she was presently receiving. There was no surrender charge for the annuity if she went into a nursing home, and she was able to use earnings from the annuity every year to pay for an insurance policy, with the church named as beneficiary. The insurance policy was available to pay accelerated benefits if needed for long term care.

RESULTS:

- She had full access to all her money for nursing home care if needed.

- The church would benefit from the annuity account for any funds not used for Long Term Care.

- The church received the proceeds of the insurance plan.

- The client received a current deduction for donating the insurance premium,

# NOW HEAR THIS!

The above illustrations are just a few examples of how an annuity account can be managed to provide maximum lifetime benefits and minimal tax loss. However, these results would not likely occur without the assistance of a qualified, conscientious and knowledgeable advisor. Annuities, like any other financial tool, need to be integrated into an overall game plan if you wish to make them work most effectively. Such planning results in the achievement of the goal of *financial peace of mind*.

One final commentary is appropriate in a chapter about making annuities work. Many times, you will receive the advice that you should consider the use of annuities only when you have exhausted all other alternatives for retirement savings. That is—you should not only maximize your 401k contributions, you should also look to setting up IRA accounts or even Roth IRA accounts before considering an annuity—or so they say!

If it is OK to place some retirement savings in a non-deductible format by utilizing a Roth IRA, what is the problem with using an annuity? Not only do you receive the same favorable tax treatment on your earnings such as a Roth IRA provides, you can bypass the legal restrictions on the Roth accounts and you are not limited in what amounts you may wish to set aside for your retirement. Even company sponsored plans are now offering the Roth IRA alternative to traditional 401k accounts, giving further evidence that there is an advantage to foregoing a current tax deduction. In other words, a conscious decision is made to use funds already taxed in order to obtain a tax benefit when the funds are actually being received. How is this any different from a plain vanilla annuity set up with a company of your own choosing?

Once again, you can assist yourself in furthering your financial game plan by working with a professional who will listen to your needs, one who is willing to place those needs ahead of 'conventional wisdom'.

# Chapter 8

# WHAT IS A CHARITABLE GIFT ANNUITY?

Here is a question for you to ponder: Your planner is aware that you are holding a block of shares from the company you were so long and faithfully employed with. These shares have grown in value and he has told you that current law allows you to pass those shares to your children and that they will not have to pay the tax on the gain under current tax laws. But, there is another opportunity to consider. If you could trade those shares worth about $100,000 for an asset that is guaranteed to be worth $250,000 to your heirs, would you do so?

*(That is correct—you trade a $100,000 account for a $250,000 account, GUARANTEED!)*

Would it affect your decision in any way if you could take a tax credit for the $100,000 by making the trade?

This is an example of what can be done with a charitable gift annuity. The subject of gifting to charities is one that is very motivational for many financial planners. The opportunity to be a hero to your favorite charity is available to the man on the street—more so than they ever have recognized.

 One of the simplest plans is the Charitable Gift Annuity (CGA). It is also one that is often overlooked by those who dismiss it as just another opportunity to give away your hard earned life savings.

By the finish of this chapter, you will hopefully understand that you do not need to deprive yourself or your heirs in order to be charitable. Indeed, there are ways in which you can actually be further ahead financially during your lifetime.

If you understand everything discussed about annuities elsewhere in this book, we need only to add one feature:

# A CHARITABLE GIFT ANNUITY IS THE ONLY NON-QUALIFIED ANNUITY THAT IS TAX DEDUCTIBLE!

The reason it is tax deductible is that it is an actual gift to a recognized charity. You can use other gifting strategies, of course, such as charitable remainder trusts, charitable lead trusts, and so on. The CGA, however, does not involve all the legalities of setting up trusts, etc. It is merely a trade of an asset for an income stream that is guaranteed to last for one or two lives. That income stream is not dependent on stock market performance.

The traded asset can be cash or a bank account, but the most effective asset to trade is one that has grown in value while held, and where there would be a substantial profit that would be taxed if that asset is sold in the marketplace. The asset could be securities, or could be a hard asset such a real estate or valuable antiques or collectables. It could also be retirement accounts such as IRA's or 401K accounts.

While for most people, the current tax on estates is not a factor, that could change with future legislation. It should be pointed out that donating assets to a charity eliminates those assets from the taxable estate.

The asset donated becomes a part of the charity's assets, and the payments are a general obligation of the charity. The annuity is backed by the charity's entire assets, not just by the property contributed. Unlike trusts, payments continue for the life or lives of the beneficiary, not ONLY as long as assets remain in the trust. The payout rates are known in advance, and can be counted on in the same manner as income from a pension or any other commercial annuity.

A person who receives payments is called an "annuitant" or "beneficiary." The payments are fixed and unchanged for the term of the contract. The annuity payments are NOT called "income," because a portion of the payments are considered to be a partial tax-free return of the donor's gift. If there is a tax liability that would be applied to the gifted asset, that liability will be spread over the life expectancy of the beneficiary. This tax effect will be offset by the tax credit taken for the gift.

The cash payment of income from these annuities can be started immediately, or it can be deferred to a date in the future, as selected by the donor. Such payments can be monthly, quarterly, semi annually, or annually.

They can also be structured to a specific need, such as payment of college tuition. A grandparent could, for example, set up a deferred arrangement for a grand child, with payments to be spread over the four or five year period starting with entrance into college. By setting up this type of a plan, it is possible for you to convert an asset with a large capital gain tax hanging overhead into a tax deductible plan for funding a college education for a favorite grandchild. (*Did you follow all that?*)

It is quite possible that your favorite charity is not set up to handle a CGA program, as there is quite an obligation on the part of the charity. This should not present a problem, however. Any qualified charity can outsource the "obligation" part of the plan to a recognized insurance company. This will require the allocation of a large portion of the gift to the insurance company, but the remainder becomes immediately available to the charity for its current financial needs.

To give an idea of the potential for those with a charitable mindset, let us take a look at some practical examples.

## COMPANY STOCK HOLDING

SITUATION: Client and his wife have company stock that has appreciated in value over the years. They figure the cost basis to be around $25,000, and the current value to be $125,000. The stocks currently pay small dividends. If sold, it would increase their taxable income by $100,000, taxed as long term gains. They would like to benefit their favorite charity, but do not wish to disinherit their children.

SOLUTION: The stock is donated to a CGA offered by their charity, resulting in a charitable deduction for tax purposes. The income is used to set up a wealth replacement plan using Life Insurance that pays off to their children when both pass on. The amount of this insurance provided at their age by the income from the CGA was $400,000.

RESULTS:

- Their charity received the $125,000 gift.
- The clients increased the amount left to their children by $275,000
- They realized an annual deduction for the gift they made.

COMMENT: This trade is only for those who have sufficient other assets for their own lifetime needs.

# INCREASING THE COMPANY PENSION

SITUATION: Similar to the prior couple, they hold a block of company stock worth about $200,000. They require more income than the 2% dividend generates. They also recognize a need for more diversification in their holdings, as they have friends whose company stock lost considerable value in the stock market. They would like to sell their stock and purchase a more secure asset to increase their income, but face a large tax liability if they sell.

SOLUTION: They donate the stock to their charity using the gift annuity plan.

RESULTS:

- They eliminate the tax barrier to selling

- They increase their income to a 7% level guaranteed for the rest of their lives

- They take a write-off from their income tax bill for several years

- The charity receives s substantial gift

COMMENT: If the couple wished to preserve the inheritance for their heirs, they could use part of the increased income to obtain wealth replacement insurance.

# THE SUCCESSFUL REAL ESTATE INVESTMENT

SITUATION: Client had the foresight some years ago to invest in a parcel of undeveloped land near a large city. He had seen the value increase from $150,000 to $500,000. He now wanted to sell the land to use the money as a retirement income, however, he wanted to minimize or avoid paying capital gains tax on his land sale.

SOLUTION: By exchanging the land for a CGA, he was able to take an immediate tax deduction for the full amount of the gift—$500,000.

RESULTS:

- He eliminated the expense of taxes on the land every year
- There was an income stream of over $35,000 instead, that would last for the life of both spouses
- There was relief from the impact of taxes on the sale of the land
- There was an annual charitable tax deduction for the gift

COMMENT: Once again if the client did not wish to "disinherit" his family, he could allocate part of the income stream from the annuity to obtain a 'wealth replacement' insurance plan. He would still have plenty of income over and above holding the vacant land without the expense of paying real estate taxes on an asset that was not meeting current goals.

NOTE: If the charity cannot take a real estate holding because of liquidity problems, there are several ways to handle it that can be found by a knowledgeable advisor.

## SOLVING THE IRA TAX DILEMMA

SITUATION: Client and his wife are both 72 years of age and have a large IRA account, and thus must take their Required Minimum Distribution, generating a large tax bill each year. They are not in need of the distribution for current income. To transfer the entire account to a Roth IRA would result in a very large tax bill with no offsetting tax credit.

SOLUTION: Transfer $50,000 each year to a CGA. Use part of the funds from the CGA to obtain a 'wealth replacement' insurance plan to go tax free to the heirs.

RESULT:

- The transfer resulted in a charitable deduction
- The deduction helped offset the income taxes on the required withdrawals
- There were no restrictions on the amount transferred as would be the case if they elected a transfer to a Roth IRA
- They met the IRS requirements for minimum annual withdrawal from the IRA
- They increased the amount payable to the heirs with the tax free benefits of the insurance plan.

The above examples are not the only ways a CGA can be utilized. They are given merely to show some typical situations that the reader can relate to. The most important ingredient for the use of a CGA is a charitable frame of mind, followed by a close working relationship with knowledgeable professional advisor.

Some years ago, in a letter to the editor, a reader observed: "Think about what local charities could accomplish if they had plenty of money to fulfill their visions. It just doesn't happen because people are uninformed." She continues: "In philanthropy, everybody wins. The donors have more money as long as one of the two spouses is alive. Heirs can actually receive a larger inheritance, and your favorite charities typically end up with more money than would have gone to Uncle Sam. It's a win-win situation." This person should be congratulated for her observations.

*All that you have shall some day be given;*

*Therefore give now, that the season of giving be yours and*

*not your inheritors.*

*From* The Prophet

*Kahlil Gibran*

# Chapter 9

# AVOIDING SURPRISES

Picture yourself having a cup of coffee in a restaurant, and you hear the sound of a jackhammer every few minutes. You ask the waitress where that sound is coming from, and she says that it is from the dentist's office upstairs. "He is running a special this week on extractions!" What is the likelihood of your taking advantage of that special?

In that same restaurant you are given a knife, a fork and a spoon. You may use the knife or fork to stir your coffee, but more likely will choose the spoon. There are also some soups you can eat with a fork, but the better choice is likely to be the spoon.

Here is the point: the jackhammer, the knife, the fork and the spoon are all tools. They each have a job to do that is most appropriate. It works the same with annuities. They are financial tools, as are bank accounts, brokerage accounts, mutual funds and investment real estate. This book merely deals with one of these tools.

The use of annuities is questioned by some people because they have heard of unexpected consequences experienced by others. Financial decisions, like prescriptions drugs, have side effects.

Insurance companies have an interest in avoiding surprises. It is just good business. In addition to providing you with an upfront "Statement of Understanding," you can now expect to be presented with a questionnaire to sign. It is designed to make sure that you have a clear idea of why you are taking the step of placing your financial welfare with such an account.

Here are some of the surprises you should be aware of:

THE 'TIME BOMB TAX' SURPRISE: Remember that taxes on gains are payable when annuities pay out benefits. In this, they are similar to IRA and 401k plans. Unlike those plans, which are 100% taxable, the annuity returns the original deposit free of taxes as a return of your deposit. To avoid this tax surprise, refer to the chapter on Super Annuities.

THE 'EARLY WITHDRAWAL' SURPRISE: Like your IRA or 401k account, there is a tax penalty for withdrawals prior to turning 59 1/2 years of age. While there are ways to offset this penalty, you should be aware of it at the time you place money into an annuity. It is the same choice you make when you put money into a regular IRA account.

THE 'ZERO INTEREST' SURPRISE: If you have a Fixed Index Annuity, there will be some years when you will receive no interest on your money. That is because the market index went down that year. You are in better shape with zero interest than the investor who saw his account value diminish with the rest of the market. (Here is one alternative for you to consider: Each anniversary you can consider telling the insurance company to place part of your account into their interest bearing alternative. That way, you will at least show some return on your money!)

THE 'SURRENDER CHARGE' SURPRISE: You find that you will incur a substantial surrender charge if you elect to liquidate the account within the first few years you hold it. The solution: Put the money someplace else to begin with. Annuities are properly used as 'long term' places for serious money. While it is possible to buy annuities with no surrender charges, this is not the normal need that annuities are designed for. Most annuities allow at least 10% access annually without imposing a surrender charge, and many waive the charge if the need arises for a nursing home or terminal illness care.

THE 'BENEFICIARY' SURPRISE: The annuity is jointly owned by a husband and wife who name their son as the primary beneficiary. When one spouse passes away, the son receives the account and not the spouse. This can be avoided by naming the 'surviving spouse' as the primary beneficiary, and the son as the contingent beneficiary. This example points out the care that should be taken in naming a beneficiary.

THE 'CASH VALUE' SURPRISE: Your beneficiaries are subject to a surrender charge when you die while the contract is in a surrender period. This is true of some contracts and not true in others. Ask before you invest.

THE 'COST OF LIVING' SURPRISE: The lifetime income you agreed to 5 years ago buys far fewer groceries these days. The solution is to arrange your payout with a plan that can offset inflation. Some fixed annuities can do this, and you can also use a Variable Annuity or a split annuity arrangement.

THE 'LOST BENEFIT' SURPRISE: Dad just passed away and his heirs found that he had invested $100,000 in a Variable Annuity that had gone down in value to $50,000 in the stock market decline following the 'dot.com' bubble. His agent advised him to wait it out and it did come up in value to about $60,000 at which time he lost patience with the market and cashed the annuity in to put the money in the bank. His heirs were thus deprived of an important benefit of variable annuities: the insurance company would have brought his account value back to $100,000 as a death benefit. Dad made a costly decision.

# SOME FINAL THOUGHTS

There have been several references made in this book pertaining to the use of annuities to pay the costs of Long Term Care Insurance premiums or Life Insurance premiums. They work as well in this respect as they do for paying for other needs in retirement. For many, there is still the question: Is Life Insurance a suitable investment for the over 60 crowd?

Most people think of Life Insurance as a way to fund a mortgage pay-off, or to replace lost income while minor children are missing the family breadwinner. When those needs are gone, there are still good reasons to consider Life Insurance. Here are just a couple:

1.  With the introduction of accelerated benefits for Long Term Care expenses, Life Insurance is no longer a die to collect proposition. Unlike regular Long Term Care plans, there is a guaranteed payoff to your heirs if you never need to go to a nursing home. This offsets the concern that paying for a separate Long Term Care policy will be a waste of money if not utilized.

2.  More and more people are coming to recognize that insurance offers an excellent way to build a legacy. Whether to fund a college education for the next generation, or to benefit a favorite charity, Life Insurance allows you to capitalize your good health in a way that other alternatives cannot do. AND, when survivorship Life Insurance is available, the results are truly amazing.

Many seniors have come to recognize that they are, in reality, managing their affairs for the benefit of their inheritors, as their own lifetime needs are well taken care of. The use of annuities as a funding medium for Life Insurance premiums offers an easy way to enhance you legacy without an added budget item. When used in conjunction with a charitable gifting program, there is also an immediate payoff in the form of an income tax reduction.

When all is said and done, you are still confronted with the real world problem of wading into the marketplace. Before doing so, you and your advisor need to do some goal analysis. In the appendices to this book, you will find forms to help you analyze your goals. If you will use them in conjunction with your advisor, you will be less likely to be surprised. It will be most helpful if you will provide him or her with a starting point, as indicated by the form in Appendix II.

Are annuities the answer to all financial situations? NO. But they are certainly not to be dismissed lightly. Over the years, they have proven to be most effective planning tools for many needs.

The aim of this book is to arm you with enough information to allow you to know what you are looking for. It hoped that this book will help you to know the merchandise, but if you still do not know the merchandise, you should know the merchant! You must still

1. Find a qualified agent, or

2. Find a reputable company

If you have never worked with a professional agent, it will be most helpful to know someone who has such a relationship and is willing to refer you to them. This is comparable to the job of finding a doctor whom you can trust. The agent you will deal with will listen to your symptoms just as a physician would, and will prescribe the best solution for you to enhance your financial health.

The image of the insurance agent is evolving from *salesperson* to *counselor*. Instead of being considered an adversary, the client and agent now sit on the same side of the table, with both focusing their attention on what best meets the client's goals and objectives. Most people recognize the value of a knowledgeable professional in this field, as they do in other areas where they cannot be expected to have expertise, such as the medical or legal fields. You certainly cannot depend on the reporting media for your guidance. Their objectives do not relate to yours. Relying on what you read in the media from reporters who have not bothered to learn the facts can be very costly.

It is very easy to find advisors who denigrate annuities. It seems to be a popular way to gather an audience. Those advisors who do so must then tell you the alternative they propose, and then it is up to you to choose which agenda you prefer. How does their package of benefits compare with those available with insurance contracts?

There are those who view any advisor as "just a salesman." However, consider this: Even a fee only planner needs to be a salesperson. The fear of dealing with a high pressure salesperson is best dealt with by being a knowledgeable consumer, and that is why this book was written.

If you want to know if the agent you are considering is a professional, here is a question you may wish to ask: "You have explained all the benefits of using annuities! Do you offer anything that will allow me to totally avoid taxes on my earnings?" If so, he will be very familiar with what is covered in the chapter on *Super Annuities*.

There are a growing number of *fee only* advisors, and there are also a large number of *no-load* devotees who shudder at the notion of paying a fee for anything (except their own fee). You need to recognize that it is not the size of the compensation your adviser receives, it is the results that count. Please refer to Chapter 7 where we speak about the lady 'Who Never Paid a Fee.'

Regarding the question of fees, here is a suggestion: LISTEN! Find out what the fees are for and then evaluate whether they provide a commensurate value. Would you prefer a no-load mutual fund with a record over time of earning a 5% return on your money, or a load fund that has a record of 10% after fees? It is no more sinful to pay a fee to an advisor than it is to go into a fancy restaurant for an excellent meal. You may pay extra to get more satisfying results.

As to the matter of finding a suitable insurance company, a good agent will be of great help. He or she can function as your search engine and thereby eliminate the job you would otherwise be forced to take on. Typically, he is looking for the same thing you are; the optimum combination of benefits, costs and choices available to fit your situation. After all, he recognizes that there are a lot of choices available for you, even if you live out in the middle of nowhere. He wants to find the solution that makes him most competitive. He certainly does not want to hook you up with a shaky company that will come back to haunt both you and him.

If you have taken the time to absorb this book, you are to be congratulated. Perhaps you still have questions—and that is understandable. Financial decision making is a fearful process for many people. But remember this: fear and ignorance do not live under the same roof. Adding knowledge should dissipate ignorance and eliminate fear. Combine the knowledge you have gained here with the knowledge and integrity of your advisor, and you will have arrived at the goal of all financial planning:

FINANCIAL PEACE OF MIND!

# APPENDIX I

# GOAL CLARIFICATION GUIDE

Goals that are important to you—Check all that apply:

_____ Lower Income tax

_____ Provide more current income

_____ Lower taxes paid on Social Security income

_____ Passing IRA or 401k in most tax efficient way

_____ Protect assets from high costs of Long Term Care

_____ Never lose any money on investments

_____ Loss of pension benefits on death of a spouse

_____ Protection of assets left to heirs

_____ Providing for grandchildren

_____ Make a lifetime gift

_____ Provide for a charitable bequest

_____ Avoid estate taxes

_____ Avoid capital gains tax

_____ Provide for children of prior marriage

_____ Provide for special needs beneficiary

_____ Keep my estate settlement private

# APPENDIX II

# STARTING POINT FOR PLANNING

WHAT I OWN:

    Bank accounts
    Checking                  _____
    Savings/CD's           _____

Retirement accounts:
    IRA                      _____
    401k/403b/TSA       _____

Real estate
    Main residence        _____
    Other real estate      _____

Investments
    Brokerage accounts    _____
    Mutual funds           _____
    Insurance/Annuities    _____
    Other                  _____

WHAT I OWE:

Home mortgage                    _____

Credit Cards                          _____

Other Obligations                  _____


Note: You will need to know how each asset is owned/titled. Is it titled in the name of a trust, in an individual's name, or in a joint account? This form is a shortened version of what an advisor will need. The more thoroughly you wish to plan, the more information will be needed.

# APPENDIX III

# BUYER'S GUIDE TO FIXED INDEXED ANNUITIES

## How do I know which Fixed Indexed Annuity is best for me?

As with any other insurance product, you must carefully consider your own personal situation and how you feel about the choices available. No single annuity design may have all the features you want. It is important to understand the features and trade-offs available so you can choose the annuity that is right for you. Keep in mind that it may be misleading to compare one annuity to another unless you compare all the other features of each annuity. You must decide for yourself what combination of features makes the most sense for you. Also, remember that it is not possible to predict the future market behavior of an index.

# QUESTIONS YOU SHOULD ASK YOUR AGENT OR THE COMPANY

- What is the guaranteed minimum interest rate?

- What charges, if any, are deducted from my premium?

- What charges, if any, are deducted from my contract value?

- How long is the term?

- What is the participation rate?

- For how long is the participation rate guaranteed?

- Is there a minimum participation rate?

- Does my contract have a cap?

- Is averaging used? How does it work?

- Is interest compounded during a term?

- Is there a margin, spread, or administrative fee? Is that in addition to or instead of a participation rate?

- Which indexing method is used in my contract?

- What are the surrender charges or penalties if I want to end my contract early and take out all of my money?

- Can I get a partial withdrawal without paying charges or losing interest? Does my contract have vesting?

- Does my annuity waive withdrawal charges if I am confined to a nursing home or diagnosed with a terminal illness?

- What annuity income payment options do I have?

- What is the death benefit?

# APPENDIX IV

# TAX DEFERRAL EXAMPLE

Consider the following numbers for a $100,000 deposit earning 5% interest in a CD and 5% interest in a tax deferred annuity. Assume a combined tax bracket of 30% throughout, using a net (after tax) return of 3.5% for the CD.

| | CD | | | | Annuity | | | |
|---|---|---|---|---|---|---|---|---|
| Year | Beginning Balance | Interest Earned | Tax Due on Interest | Balance After Tax | Starting Balance | Interest Earned | Tax Deferred Balance | Annuity Advantage |
| 1 | 100,000 | 5,000 | 1,500 | 103,500 | 100,000 | 5,000 | 105,000 | 1,500 |
| 2 | 103,500 | 5,175 | 1,553 | 107,123 | 105,000 | 5,250 | 110,250 | 3,128 |
| 3 | 107,123 | 5,356 | 1,607 | 110,872 | 110,250 | 5,513 | 115,763 | 4,891 |
| 4 | 110,872 | 5,544 | 1,663 | 114,752 | 115,763 | 5,788 | 121,551 | 6,798 |
| 5 | 114,752 | 5,738 | 1,721 | 118,769 | 121,551 | 6,078 | 127,628 | 8,860 |
| 6 | 118,769 | 5,938 | 1,782 | 122,926 | 127,628 | 6,381 | 134,010 | 11,084 |
| 7 | 122,926 | 6,146 | 1,844 | 127,228 | 134,010 | 6,700 | 140,710 | 13,482 |
| 8 | 127,228 | 6,361 | 1,908 | 131,681 | 140,710 | 7,036 | 147,746 | 16,065 |
| 9 | 131,681 | 6,584 | 1,975 | 136,290 | 147,746 | 7,387 | 155,133 | 18,843 |
| 10 | 136,290 | 6,814 | 2,044 | 141,060 | 155,133 | 7,757 | 162,889 | 21,830 |
| 11 | 141,060 | 7,053 | 2,116 | 145,997 | 162,889 | 8,144 | 171,034 | 25,037 |
| 12 | 145,997 | 7,300 | 2,190 | 151,107 | 171,034 | 8,552 | 179,586 | 28,479 |
| 13 | 151,107 | 7,555 | 2,267 | 156,396 | 179,586 | 8,979 | 188,565 | 32,169 |
| 14 | 156,396 | 7,820 | 2,346 | 161,869 | 188,565 | 9,428 | 197,993 | 36,124 |
| 15 | 161,869 | 8,093 | 2,428 | **167,535** | 197,993 | 9,900 | **207,893** | **40,358** |

Taxable

Gain: 107,893

Note the Values in 15 years:          CD          $167,535

                                      Annuity      $207,893

The Annuity account is worth <u>$40,358</u> more by taking advantage of tax deferral.

## INCOME COMPARISON

If, at the end of 15 years, you take an 8% income from either, here is the annual income:

                    CD          $13,402

                    Annuity      $16,632

You have increased your income by 24% by using tax deferral. A portion of the annuity income would be considered return of principal if an annuity option is elected.

## FULL LIQUIDATION SCENARIO

If you fully liquidate the CD in 15 years, you pay no tax because you have already paid the taxes over the years.

With the annuity, you have a taxable gain of $107,893 on which you need to pay the tax, which in a 30% bracket will be $32,367. Even after paying the tax, you have almost $8,000 more left over in comparison to the CD that has already been taxed.

CPSIA information can be obtained at www.ICGtesting.com
Printed in the USA
BVOW07s0133210813

329154BV00001B/135/A